Praise for *We H*

"David, through his deeply personal words to his family and community, masterfully calls our attention to the systemic injustices that perpetuate themselves under the false promises of the American Dream; offered only to some, invisibly blocked to others. We, the witnesses and fellow victims to this truth cannot look away—we must not. *Maraming salamat*, E. J., for your vulnerability and courage. May it serve to grow the awareness necessary to shift the trajectory of our future ancestors' experiences."

— Jorie Ayyu Paoli, Vice President and Indigenous Operations Director, First Alaskans Institute

"David is gifted with the wisdom and philosophical acumen of an Elder. I emerged from the deep, dark truths about the aftermath of colonialism emanating from David's heart with an amplified sense of urgency to instill hope, resilience, and belief in current and coming generations that this world can and will be 'a better place.'"

— Pausauraq Jana Harcharek, Director of Iñupiaq Education, North Slope Borough School District

"David has written a spiritual, self-examination, and cultural critique of his American and his Filipino family. It reminds me of the duality of Black consciousness elegantly depicted by W. E. B. Dubois. In the final summation, he exhorts his native family to love and believe in themselves, to shed the idea that they are special because of their Americanness, and to reclaim their *kapwa*—their humanity. He also challenges

White America to find theirs. David has rendered a powerful and valuable meditation, guided by self-reflection and familial love, and grounded in intellectual discernment and a generosity of spirit. An inspiring and informative read."

— James M. Jones, author of
Prejudice and Racism, Second Edition

"This book is a heartbreaking and heart-validating masterpiece about a Filipino American immigrant man who worries about the future of his children in what was once deemed a 'post-racial' America. In his letters to his family, he tackles a spectrum of issues affecting people of color—from unlawful police deaths to historical trauma to immigration reform. His intersectional lens in understanding how his own multiracial kids may be forced to overcome obstacles like colonial mentality, toxic masculinity, institutional sexism, and stereotype threat is one that is rare, raw, and refreshing for an academic. He brilliantly uses personal stories, historical facts, and contemporary media accounts, while tying in scientific psychological and epidemiological research, to demonstrate how racism, classism, sexism, heterosexism, and other forms of oppression are slowly killing us. In sharing the grief, anger, and trauma of losing his childhood friend to unjust police violence, his voice becomes one that represents the weight that 'woke' Black and Brown Americans carry with us daily, as we continue to survive, thrive, and tremble in this society."

— Kevin L. Nadal, author of *Filipino American Psychology: A Handbook of Theory, Research, and Clinical Practice*

"David takes often theoretical constructs such as 'internal oppression,' 'white privilege,' 'historical trauma,' and provides visceral, emotional contexts through examination of his own personal life and the lives of his loved ones, both ancestral and current. He delivers those contexts through well-crafted letters to his wife, sons, and daughter explaining the complexities of their realities in an approachable, easy-to-understand manner. One of David's most striking analyses is bridging the perceived gulf between Native Americans and his status as a Filipino who immigrated to Native American lands. This is an important work that ties together histories, generations, and peoples and provides the reader with a solid grounding to challenge the dominant narrative."

— Bonnie Duran, Indigenous Wellness Research Institute, University of Washington

"History is about stories of conquests through the ages. Historians often write those stories with a dispassionate view of colonization and oppression. E. J. R. David's book gives a personal narrative on topics of oppression and racism to his family. It's also a gift to others whose voices have been muted. 'Letters' to his family is a time capsule worth reexamining."

— Jim "Aqpayuq" W. LaBelle

WE HAVE NOT STOPPED TREMBLING YET

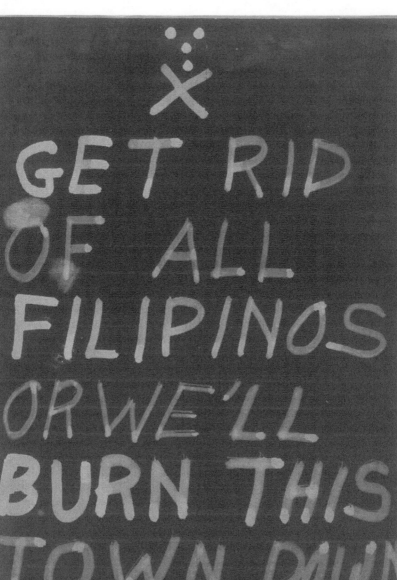

WE HAVE NOT STOPPED TREMBLING YET

LETTERS TO MY FILIPINO-ATHABASCAN FAMILY

E. J. R. DAVID

Cover image and frontispiece: [Get rid of all Filipinos or we'll burn this town down letter], James Earl Wood collection on Filipinos in California, BANC MSS C-R 4, Box 2, Folder 18. Courtesy of The Bancroft Library, University of California, Berkeley.

Published by State University of New York Press, Albany

© 2018 State University of New York

For information, contact State University of New York Press,
Albany, NY
www.sunypress.edu

Production, Ryan Morris
Marketing, Fran Keneston
Book design, Aimee Harrison

Library of Congress Cataloging-in-Publication Data

Names: David, E. J. R. (Eric John Ramos), author.
Title: We have not stopped trembling yet : letters to my Filipino-Athabascan
    family / E. J. R. David.
Other titles: Letters to my Filipino-Athabascan family
Description: Albany, NY : State University of New York Press, [2018] |
    Includes bibliographical references.
Identifiers: LCCN 2017027514 | ISBN 9781438469522 (pbk. : alk. paper) |
    ISBN 9781438469539 (e-book)
Subjects: LCSH: David, E. J. R. (Eric John Ramos) | Filipino Americans—
    Alaska—Biography. | Filipino Americans—Ethnic identity. | Athapascan
    Indians—Ethnic identity. | Athapascan Indians—Alaska—Biography. |
    Racism—United States—21st century. | Alaska—Race relations.
Classification: LCC F915.F4 D38 2018 | DDC 305.8009798—dc23
LC record available at https://lccn.loc.gov/2017027514

10 9 8 7 6 5 4 3 2 1

For Margaret, Laka, Manu, and Kalu.
You all teach me so much.

For Pamiuq's family.
Quyanaqpak for blessing us with Pum.

CONTENTS

The stories in this book reflect the author's recollection of events. Although the stories are verifiable by publicly available and well-circulated sources, some names, locations, and other identifying information have nevertheless been changed to respect the privacy of those depicted. The presented dialogues in various parts of the book have been re-created based on the author's memory.

PREFACE

Dear Reader,

This book is nonfiction. Although some identifying details have been changed, the stories I share in the letters are real and, consequently, so are the emotions, insecurities, and confused thoughts that I experienced. However, this is not a memoir. Although race, racism, and other forms of oppression—historically and contemporarily—are important and defining components of my life, they do not make up the entirety of who I am. Also, these letters were written as expressions of my struggles, anger, and anxieties that became especially salient during a particularly dark moment of my life—a moment sparked by the painfully tragic death of one of my best friends. Although some of my convictions and perspectives may have changed since these letters were written—attesting to the state-dependence of extreme emotions, the ups and downs of life, the natural trajectory of growth and maturity, as well as the reality that racial identity development is never-ending so long as we are living and interacting with this racialized world—many of my viewpoints shared in this book have remained the same and will most likely remain the same forever. In fact, I have expressed similar perspectives about these same topics in my previous works prior to writing these letters. Further, I also want to note that, in each of the letters I explore a set of issues or themes not necessarily because they apply only to the person to whom I am writing in the particular letter—although this is sometimes the case—but also because I felt that there are certain topics that are more organically fitting to explore with a particular person compared to others. For example, just because I am discussing a certain issue with my daughter does not necessarily mean that the issue does not apply to my sons, and vice versa; it's just that some topics more naturally come up in some conversations than others. Finally, although these letters were intended for my family, I know that the issues I have been struggling with are much bigger than me and my loved ones. Therefore, each of the letters is written to address broader themes that open up the conversation to many others who may share similar experiences. I hope other folks are somehow able to relate and connect.

To you and other folks who come across this book—I offer kamalayan, kapwa, lakas, kalayaan, and kaluguran.

Maraming salamat—thank you—for your time and open hearts.

In kapwa,

E. J. R. David

PROLOGUE

Barrow Whalers high school basketball team photo when Pum was a senior and E.J. was a junior. Circa 1998.

It was summer of 1998 in Barrow, Alaska. Pum just graduated from high school and I was waiting for my senior year to start. I realized that I had one more year, and then I had to do something with my life. Knowing that I had no money for college and that I did not have any other options, I decided to enlist in the United States Army. So I called Pum.

> E.J.: Hey, I'm thinking of joining the Army.
> PUM: Okay. I'll go with you.

For real, it was that simple. It was that easy.

A few days later, Pum and I traveled to Anchorage together to complete the paperwork, do the medical and physical examinations, and get ready for basic training. Because he was already done with high school, he was ready to go ahead with basic training and start his life with the Army. I, on the other hand, still had to finish my senior year. The plan was for me to go to basic training right after graduating from high school. So Pum and I talked.

> E.J.: Is that cool man? I'll follow you in the Army, for real, then we'll be in it together.
> PUM: Yeah, no problem.

For real. It was that simple. It was that easy.

So Pum went ahead and started his Army service, and I went into my last year of high school with a strong sense of purpose. During my senior year, however, other opportunities became available for me. One day, I called Pum and nervously and embarrassingly said the following:

> **E.J.:** Hey bro, I got a scholarship to go to college. I think I am going to have to back out of my Army commitment. Sorry.
>
> **PUM:** What are you saying sorry for? You take advantage of that scholarship and put it to good use. I'm good here. The Army is good for me. Thank you for bringing me in it.

For real. It was that simple. It was that easy.

You see, that's the kind of friend Pum is—or was. He was loyal. He was for life. He was real. He was genuine. It was easy to be his friend. We didn't have to work hard for our friendship—our brotherhood—because it was real.

It was easy and it was simple, because it was real.

The years passed and my brother Pum and I took different paths, but our bond and loyalty to each other never weakened. Over the years we matured, we learned, we got married, we had kids, we grew, but we did not grow apart. I'm not going to lie, Pum and I did not agree on everything—especially politics—but we loved each other. We respected each other. We cheered for each other. We supported each other. Still. For real. It was that simple. It was that easy.

Then, very early on the morning of February 10, 2016, my phone rang. It was my other brother.

> **DONOVAN:** Hey bro, Aunt Flossie and Uncle Roy called. I just got off the phone with them . . .

Right now, the anger and sadness and confusion and regret and doubt and pain that I and Pum's family, friends, and community are going through is too complex and too difficult.

For real. This is not simple. This is not easy.

I. MY AMERICAN FAMILY

We are all Americans that have toiled and suffered and known oppression and defeat, from the first Indian that offered peace in Manhattan to the last Filipino pea pickers. America is not bound by geographical latitudes. America is not merely a land or an institution. America is in the hearts of men (and women) that died for freedom; it is also in the eyes of men (and women) that are building a new world.... America is also the nameless foreigner, the homeless refugee, the hungry boy begging for a job and the black body dangling from a tree. America is the illiterate immigrant who is ashamed that the world of books and intellectual opportunities is closed to him. We are that nameless foreigner, that homeless refugee, that hungry boy, that illiterate immigrant and that lynched black body. All of us, from the first Adams to the last Filipino, native born or alien, educated or illiterate—We are America!

—Carlos Bulosan (1946),
America Is in the Heart: A Personal History

A section of E.J.'s birth certificate indicating his parents', and therefore his, nationality and race.

March 16, 2016

My American Family,

You all know that Pamiuq, one of my best friends from Barrow, just died last month. You know that he was shot and killed by a police officer. You also know that this happened while Pum was in his own house, alone, and that Pum's wife told the police officers to just leave Pum alone. Pum wasn't threatening to hurt anyone. In fact, he even told the police—very clearly—that they had no right to enter his house.

But the police barged in anyway. I wonder how different the outcome could have been if the police had stayed outside and negotiated with Pum, like they seem to do in other similar cases. In fact, just a few weeks after Pum's tragic death, there was a man in Bethel who was alone in his house with a gun, threatening to shoot police and children. The police negotiated with him for thirty-one hours, and the police also requested a Southcentral Special Emergency Reaction Team and relief negotiators from Anchorage. The man eventually surrendered, and is still alive.

I wonder how different things could've been if Barrow police stayed outside, de-escalated the situation, waited and negotiated even for just one hour. Even for just thirty minutes. I wonder how different things could've been if a Southcentral Special Emergency Reaction Team and relief negotiators were flown in from Anchorage or Fairbanks to help Pum. I wonder if things would have turned out differently for Pum. I wonder.

It's not a surprise to you all how deeply affected and troubled I am by Pum's death. He was my brother. He was me. On the surface, Pum and I may not seem to have much in common. He's Inupiaq; indigenous to these lands. He's also very Republican. On the other hand, I am a Filipino immigrant to this country. And I am not Republican.

Our differences end here, however, as Pum was thirty-six years and four months old when he died, and I am only three months younger than him. He and I cut each other's hair, and gave each other fades. He and I got drunk and freestyle rapped together, badly, many times. He and I shot ducks together. He and I listened to the Wu-Tang Clan together. He and I went to high school together, played in the same basketball team together, and began to grow older together as we matured and started our own families.

He married a Filipina immigrant who was from the same region in the Philippines as my ancestors, and together they have "Eskipino" kids.

And especially in this sense, Pum is—or was— very much just like me. His family is very much just like our family.

You are all Koyukon Athabascans—indigenous to these lands, just like Pum. My love, you have me as a husband, and—Malakas, Kalayaan, and Kaluguran—the three of you kids have me as a father: a Filipino immigrant. The three of you are "Filibascans," similar to Pum's kids.

And so Pum passing away, and my thinking about this tragedy's effect on his wife and his children, naturally led me to thinking about you. Right now, I am merely two months away from being the same age he was when he got shot. What if something happens to me? What if I passed away suddenly and unexpectedly, perhaps even tragically? How would that affect you?

But my question evolved the more I thought about it. Instead of focusing on how my death might affect you, I began to think about how I should prepare you for the reality that I am going to pass away—perhaps suddenly and unexpectedly and, conceivably, tragically too.

To prepare you for my death, I began to think of the possible risk-factors and threats to my life. I began to think about all the elements that have shaped my life: my habits, my behaviors, my thoughts, my self-esteem, my health. I thought about the factors that have influenced how I've lived my life and so, naturally, I began to think about the factors that may conceivably contribute to my death.

But for me to be completely real, I realized that I cannot just tell you what happened to me directly. I also need to tell you what happened to my parents who produced and raised me, because their experiences shaped them and their shape molded me. I also need to tell you about the generations before, and what happened to them. I need to tell you about our ancestors, what they had and what was violently taken away from them, for you to completely understand the factors that played a role in my life, and therefore, the factors that will play a role in my death.

And as I thought about how the experiences of my ancestors affect me, my question evolved yet again: I began to think about how my experiences will also affect you as my kids! The three of you are products of me, and my shape will shape you. So these same factors—the risk factors for my death—will be the same for you. So understanding what shaped my life and what may lead to my death will also help you completely grasp the factors that may likewise play a role in your own lives, and therefore, your own deaths.

And this is true for you too, my love. As my partner, factors that affect my life and contribute to my death undoubtedly affect you too, vicariously and distally, but nevertheless still very true.

I hope that by understanding these risk factors better, by at least becoming aware of them, perhaps you can do things now to prevent them. Perhaps you can do things now to address them, to eliminate them. So that—maybe—you can lessen the risk factors in your own lives, lessen the factors that may contribute to your own deaths. So that—maybe—you can lighten the burdens of death that you inherited from me. Then—maybe, hopefully—you will pass on something better to the next generations.

To impact the current, younger, and future generations, I need to go into some history because, as a brown-skinned immigrant man in this country, my reality is different, and it's different because of the historical and contemporary oppression that people like me have experienced. I will probably get redundant, my loves, because oppression is redundant. Oppression has redundantly damaged our Peoples for generations! What our ancestors faced affect us and what we face will affect the future generations. And guess what? What we do with our own lives, our own chance, our own shot, can affect our ancestors as well. You see,

Peoples of Color like me—like us—are connected to our families and our ancestors in a very deep, real way. I don't mean this in a metaphorical, abstract, mystical way. This connection to our ancestors is real. It's tangible. It's visible. You can feel it; all of it. You can feel the joys, but you can also feel the pains.

And I hope these letters help you understand how this is so.

My American family, I am an immigrant, unlike all of you. My first language is not English, unlike all of you. I am brown skinned, darker than all of you. I am a settler in this country, perhaps contributing to the neocolonial oppression of my own family—my own blood—as all four of you are indigenous to these lands.

I am still struggling with this, still trying to resolve this internal conflict between my "settler colonialist" identity and my "victim of colonization" reality. Perhaps I will never resolve it, but let me tell you a little bit about my confusions and why I am struggling. Let me tell you a little bit about why I am not the only one responsible for becoming a settler in these lands. Let me tell you about why my ancestors believed that they are connected to these lands, why they fantasized about coming to these lands, why they felt the need to send me to these lands.

My indigenous lands are now called the Philippines, its colonial name, an archipelago of over 7,000 tropical islands in the Pacific Ocean. My ancestors are from a region in northern Philippines, and they are called Kapampangan—which means people of the riverbanks, and Tagalog—which means people of the river. My first language is Tagalog, which is why my grammar is still messed up, why I still mispronounce some English words, why my accent still slips out occasionally, why I still mix up my *p*'s and *f*'s, and why I still mix up *he* and *she*, things that make you giggle sometimes.

As I write this, there is an ugly and hateful discourse about immigration in our country, about people with different birth origins, different cultures, different upbringings, different languages, and different accents—people like me. The Republican frontrunner to become the next president of our country is winning because of—again, *because of* and not *despite of*—his explicitly racist and bigoted views against immigrants, against people who are like me.

Not very many people know this, as the national immigration debate tends to be limited to Mexicans and people from Central America, but over 1.8 million out of the 3.5 million people with Filipino heritage in the United States are foreign born. This makes Filipinos the fourth-largest American immigrant group next to Mexicans, Asian Indians, and Chinese, and makes Filipinos the second-largest Asian group in the country after the Chinese. And as recently as 2010, Filipinos were the second largest immigrant group in the country after Mexicans.

In our home state of Alaska, around 9 percent of the population are foreign-born, a relatively low proportion compared to the national average, which shows that 13 percent of the American population are foreign-born. So yes, it is still relatively rare to find a foreign-born Alaskan, like me. Like your Lola and Uncle Bonz. Like your Uncle Pum's wife and her family.

But don't let this fool you into thinking that Alaska is not racially and culturally diverse! Next to Hawaii, our home state is probably the second-most racially diverse state in the country. In fact, the most racially diverse neighborhood in the country is in Anchorage—not in Queens, not in Los Angeles, not in Honolulu. Consistent with this finding that seems to surprise everyone else except Alaskans, the top three most racially diverse public high schools in the United States are in Anchorage. Furthermore, the top four—and six of the top ten—most racially diverse public middle schools in the country are also in Anchorage. Even further, the top nineteen out of the twenty most racially diverse public elementary schools in the United States are in Anchorage!

A big reason for this awesome diversity in Alaska is the large number of Asians in the state, as they are now the third-largest racial group in Alaska after Whites and Natives. Although it is not until the year 2065 that experts project Asians will surpass Latinos as America's largest immigrant group, this is already the case for Alaska right now. This is one of the very few areas wherein Alaska is not behind the rest of the country, as many Alaskans seem to complain habitually. In this case, Alaska is actually fifty years ahead of the rest of the United States.

A big reason for why Asians are the largest immigrant group in Alaska is the state's large population of Filipino Americans, whose presence in Alaska goes all the way back to 1788. So there have been many other mixed-race Alaska Native-Filipino people like you—Malakas Kalayaan, Kaluguran—who were born out of the unions of sojourning Filipino fishermen and Alaska Native women. That's pretty cool, isn't it?

Today, approximately half of the Asian population in Alaska is Filipino; the other twelve-plus Asian ethnic groups split the remaining half. This easily makes Filipinos the largest Asian Pacific Islander group in the state. Filipinos are also the largest Asian group in the most populated state of California, as well as in Arizona, Hawaii, Idaho, Montana, Nevada, New Mexico, Washington, Wyoming, and South Dakota. Also, unlike most other states where Mexicans make up the largest immigrant ethnic group, Filipinos are the largest immigrant ethnic group in Alaska. Not surprisingly, Filipinos are also the largest undocumented immigrant group in Alaska. Nationally, very few people know that Filipinos compose the biggest undocumented immigrant population in the United States after Mexicans, El Salvadorians, Guatemalans, and Hondurans.

And today it is a Filipino undocumented immigrant who has brought mainstream national attention to immigration issues.

Jose Antonio Vargas was born in the Philippines in the 1980s, just like me. Then, when he was a child, he was sent by his mother to the United States. I, too, was sent by your Lola to the United States when I was a child. But unlike Jose Antonio, I happened to have the proper documentation. My American family, I need you all to understand that although millions of others are not as lucky as I am to have papers, their lives and experiences are not of any less value.

You see, I didn't earn those documents. I didn't work for them. I was just privileged to have them. Just like you, and how you didn't earn or work for the privilege of being a United States citizen; you are simply privileged to have been born with it.

You all need to understand this, to appreciate this, so that you don't buy into yet another manner of separating yourself from others. There's already too many ways to do that. This country has already created too many ways of dividing people, attaching desirable and undesirable connotations to the created groups, giving some groups privileges while denying it to others, and arranging the groups hierarchically. You need to know this, my loves, and you need to resist this.

✦ ✦ ✦

Over the past couple of years, since Jose Antonio came out about his undocumented status, he has exposed the holes of our immigration policies, revealing the enormity and complexity of the issue. This has led to a lot of mainstream attention, like the wide-scale coverage on the "border children" from Central America—many of whom are around the same age as you, Malakas, Kalayaan, Kaluguran. Even more recently, immigration has been a central topic of the presidential campaign, and the fears about letting "terrorists who hate America" into our borders have permeated our daily climate.

The sheer attention and passion that millions of Americans have devoted to this issue tell us that the need for comprehensive immigration reform has become apparent and imperative. But, my American family, the reforms cannot simply be about building walls or tightening border security or mass deportation or other exclusionary acts—there's nothing comprehensive about such "solutions." For immigration reform to be comprehensive, I need you to understand that the process needs to consider and incorporate the fact that America—or more specifically, our foreign policies and impositions on various countries in the past and in modern times—are also parts of the "immigration problem."

Let me be clearer and more explicit: Americans themselves are parts—big parts—of the "immigration problem."

There is nothing new or radical about this statement, and the evidence for this is quite simple. You just need to understand that America "went there" first.

Jose Antonio's case and the Filipino experience is one example. He was educated in the United States, has paid taxes, employed Americans, and contributed to the common good. Although he is not a United States citizen, the United States has been his home for more than twenty years—and given the United States' long military, political, economic, and cultural involvement in the Philippines—America definitely has always been in Jose Antonio's heart. My American family, America has always been in many Filipinos' hearts—for many generations.

You see, Spain colonized the Philippines for almost 350 years, instilling a Western and White ideal among Filipinos. Then, after Filipinos fought for, died for, and won their freedom from Spain, the United States snuck in and colonized the Philippines in 1898, and established a nationwide school system that inculcated Filipinos with American standards and worldviews.

It's important for you to know that Filipinos didn't just welcome the United States with open arms, calling out to be saved, educated, and civilized.

My ancestors desperately attempted to keep their independence from being taken away by the United States during the Philippine-American War, a war that cost the United States around $600 million—which is huge for early 1900s money—and approximately 10,000 soldiers—which is always tragic regardless of the time period. Among Filipinos, it has been estimated that around 16,000 soldiers and 200,000 civilians were killed between 1899 and 1902. And although the war was declared to have been won by the United States in 1902, my ancestors continued to fight and resist America's illegal presence in the islands until 1913, a brutal fifteen-year period that includes the infamous Moro Crater Massacre in 1906, when hundreds of civilians, women, and children were executed by American soldiers. Some experts have estimated that about one-and-a-half-million people who were native to the islands died as a result of American occupation of the Philippines between 1898 and 1913, leading some scholars to conclude that Filipinos experienced genocide at the hands of Americans!

Doesn't it make you wonder why such a bloody, traumatic, and costly—in terms of money but more importantly in terms of lives lost—fifteen-year period of American history that includes ethnic and cultural genocide is not widely known? Why is this not taught in schools? Do we not remember and honor the soldiers and the civilians who lost their lives during this war?

The historical amnesia—or should I say selective amnesia—regarding this war is perplexing, because it got quite the national attention during the early 1900s. This war was so brutal and controversial that many Americans, led by Mark Twain and the Anti-Imperialist League, were criticizing America's presence in the Philippines, questioning why so much money and so many lives were being lost in the Pacific islands. As a response, President William McKinley used the ideas of Manifest Destiny and Benevolent Assimilation to defend his motivation and intentions for colonizing the Philippines, explaining "that there was nothing left for us to do but to take them all, and to educate the Filipinos, and uplift and civilize and Christianize them."

President McKinley wasn't the only American leader who held such inferiorizing sentiments about Filipinos, with Republican Senator Albert Beveridge of Indiana providing the following rationale for why the United States needed to colonize the Philippines and its Peoples:

> We must remember that we are not dealing with Americans or Europeans... We are dealing with Orientals who are Malays. They mistake kindness for weakness, forbearance for fear. It could not be otherwise unless you could erase hundreds of years of savagery... They are not capable of self-government. How could they be? They are not of a self-governing race... Savage blood, Oriental blood, Malay blood, Spanish example—are these the elements of self-government? We must never forget that in dealing with the Filipinos we deal with children.

You need to know that many Americans, including their highest leaders such as its senators and even its president, saw Filipinos as inferior. They saw Filipinos like me as childlike, unenlightened, and as dirty savages, and that it was their benevolent duty—their rightful destiny—to give me my first bath using the waters of civilization and the brush of education.

Even though my ancestors had already declared their independence, developed a constitution, and elected their leaders before the United States even got there, Filipinos were still perceived as not civilized enough to govern themselves. Even though most of my ancestors were already Christians before Americans even got to the islands, the United States still felt that it was their manifest duty to "Christianize" my Peoples. Even though the Philippines already had a well-established university—the University of Santo Thomas was founded in 1611—long before the first American university was established—Harvard was founded in 1636—the United States still felt that it was their destiny and benevolent burden to educate my Peoples. America's demeaning view and conduct toward my ancestors are similar to how African Americans and America's First Peoples were perceived and treated by the United States, as noted by ethnic studies scholar Yen Le Espiritu:

> Theodore Roosevelt ... repeatedly linked Native Americans to Filipinos, employing words like "wild and ignorant," "savages," "Apaches," and "Sioux" to refer to the Filipino people. In the same way, white American soldiers in the Philippines used many of the same epithets to describe Filipinos as they used to describe African Americans, including "niggers," "black devils," and "gugus" ... If we positioned Filipino/American history within the traditional immigration paradigm, we would miss the ethnic and racial intersections between Filipinos and Native Americans and African Americans as groups similarly affected by the forces of Manifest Destiny. These common contexts

of struggle were not lost on African American soldiers in the Philippines. Connecting their fight against domestic racism to the Filipino struggle against U.S. imperialism, some African American soldiers—such as Corporal David Fagen—switched allegiance and joined the native armed struggle for independence.

My American family, I hope that you see the similarities and links between America's First Peoples, African Americans, and Filipinos—similarities that are lost in popular presentations of American history and even Filipino history, which often simplistically portray Filipinos as one of the largest "voluntary immigrant" groups in the United States. And I am forever thankful and indebted to the leadership of the Native American and African American communities, and the struggles and movements of our Native and Black brothers and sisters—struggles and movements that many of them literally lost their lives for—because it is their work that woke me up to the complex truths of Filipinos' relationship with the United States. This true history reveals to us that, similar to the experiences of our Native and Black kapwa, it was not the Filipinos who initiated contact and tried to begin a relationship with the United States; it was the other way around through American colonialism, imperialism, and oppression!

The true history also reveals to us that, similar to what the United States did to America's First Peoples and African Americans, the Filipino culture and body were also systematically degraded and inferiorized using the ideas of Manifest Destiny and Benevolent Assimilation as the primary motivators and rationale. Unfortunately, very few bothered to pay serious attention to the flip side of these ideas—that for Americans to see themselves as being responsible for civilizing the rest of the world, they also had to believe that everyone else was inferior and uncivilized. Or maybe people did see this flip side; they just bought into it and believed it. Perhaps White Americans have developed internalized superiority to justify their oppression of other people, to make themselves feel good about the injustices and inequalities they create.

One of the more egregious attempts to convince Americans of their superiority over Filipinos, demonstrate the savagery and uncivilized nature of my ancestors, and rationalize America's civilization and benevolent intention in the Philippines took place when the United States brought 1,200 Filipinos to the St. Louis World's Fair in 1904, and sequestered them in what was called "The Philippine Reservation." This forty-seven-acre exhibit presented a range of Filipino "civilization levels," with Aetas and other indigenous tribes being portrayed as the most savage and American-trained Filipino soldiers being the most civilized. A poster advertising this human display stated that it included 40 different Native Filipino tribes, 6 "Philippine villages," 70,000 exhibits, 130 buildings. Further, the poster boasted that the Filipino exhibit was "The overshadowing feature of the world's fair," and that it was "Better than a trip through the Philippine islands." The exhibit was very popular, as Americans curiously watched, observed, and inspected the captured Filipinos as if they were a display of animals in a zoo.

So my American family, you need to know that America wanted so badly to be in the Philippines that it spent millions and lost many of its citizens' lives to get to the islands. It was as if America had a "I gotta get to the Philippines and colonize and control it, even if it means killing millions of people and spending millions of dollars" instinct. Perhaps this intrinsic motivation was due to Manifest Destiny, to America's distorted sense of superiority. We know now, though, that there were also external motivations; that America occupied the Philippines to exploit my homelands' resources—including its Peoples and its strategically advantageous geographic location—to benefit America. We know now that my Peoples were used as the primary source of cheap labor for the fields of Hawaii, California, Oregon, and Washington, as well as for the canneries of Alaska. And we know now that after America got what it wanted, then all of a sudden it discarded the Philippines, developed laws to send Filipinos in America back to the Philippines, and established policies to keep Filipinos from coming into the United States. We know now that America was violently and deviously built in large part on my Peoples' backs.

My American family, my mixed-heritage Athabascan-Filipino family, it is important to me that you know this history. You need to be aware of the fact that the United States owned and controlled, used and abused, ravaged and exploited the Philippines and its peoples—my Peoples.

And you need to be aware that such ugly and painful experiences are going to be hidden and erased from our collective memories, and you need to resist this amnesia. You need to know that Filipino banishment goes back to the fact that there was a Philippine-American War that lasted for fifteen years and during which thousands—some say one-and-a-half million—Filipinos were killed by Americans, yet such a war seems to be unacknowledged, hidden, and forgotten. You need to know that Filipino marginalization goes back to the days of the manong generation, whose struggles in the farms of Hawaii, California, and Washington—as well as in the canneries of Alaska—continue to be unknown to many. It goes back to how the hard work and leadership of Larry Itliong, Philip Vera Cruz, and other Filipino farmworkers were overshadowed by the celebrity of Cesar Chavez. You need to know that the dehumanization of Filipino Americans and the devaluation of their lives go back to the early to mid-1900s, when mobs of White men bombed, torched, and threw dynamites into buildings where Filipinos lived, worked, and played—and how White men shot, maimed, burned to death, beat to death, and hanged Filipinos—yet no one seems to remember nor care. It goes back to how President Franklin Roosevelt pledged that Filipinos who fought for the United States during World War II would be granted citizenship and military benefits—so over 250,000 Filipinos heeded the call—but shortly after the war ended that promise was taken back with the Rescission Act of 1946. You need to know that the willful ignorance and forgetting of Filipinos goes back to the many ways in which Filipino people have contributed to this country's rise as a global power, but the American masses remain oblivious to such historical and contemporary reality.

You need to remember that a part of your identity— the American, privileged part of yourselves—exploited, dehumanized, and inferiorized my Peoples, my ancestors, me. You need to know and remember that the American part of yourselves oppressed another part of you, so that you are always reminded that—despite the loud proclamations of American exceptionalism—America was not, is not, and has never been perfect. Please don't ever believe the notion that being American makes you superior to others, or that you are perfect. My loves, American superiority is a delusion; we are not perfect.

✦ ✦ ✦

The ugly legacies of America's imperfection continue to be strong in the islands to this day, despite the fact that the United States "gave" the Philippines its independence back in 1946. You can see evidence of this sad reality very easily today, with the continued presence of American soldiers in the Philippines to "train" Filipino soldiers in suppressing terrorism, insurgency, and foreign threats, and the continued use of English as the primary language in Philippine education, law, government, business, and science. Also, Filipino schools today—like the nursing programs, for example—are designed to meet the needs, certifications, and cultural mores of Western nations such as the United States and Canada, making it the norm for Filipinos to dream for and work toward jobs in Western countries. Did you know that the Philippines is the world's largest supplier of nurses? Did you know that the Philippines's biggest export is its people?

And even among those who do not leave the Philippines, many are still working for—or serving—the United States as American-owned businesses continue to outsource jobs to the Philippines. My Ate—my older sister—has been with such a company for years now, and she tells me about calling people in Iowa and chatting with them about the winter and the recent tornado, giving Americans the impression that she is located locally in Iowa, or at least, somewhere in the United States. American companies love to outsource to the Philippines because of Filipinos' high level of English proficiency and familiarity with American culture. So the cycle goes like this: Filipinos need jobs to survive, and plenty of the jobs are for companies that cater to the United States; in order to get these jobs, Filipinos need to be proficient in English and become Americanized; and so Filipinos end up hiding, ignoring, and forgetting—many times even denigrating and hating—their own languages and cultures in the process, so that they can get these jobs. As Filipino American rapper Bambu shared in his collaboration with Prometheus Brown:

> *I'm from a place where the system's still feudal, and the*
> *masses still colonized*
> *Landlord's light skinned, stabbin' with their colored eyes*
> *Wonder why the goods ain't no good, so we import*
> *Things we can make our damn selves, and we export*
> *Fleshbone, sister tryna make it home paid*
> *While my privilege let me look at my plate, and complain*

My loves, Filipinos today literally have to be Americanized to survive. Filipinos literally have to shed their Filipino-ness—or at least hide it—to survive. And I am talking about Filipinos in the Philippines, a place that is supposedly their own; land that is supposedly free and independent from America. So, yes, my American family, today we see that the Filipino culture and body are still being vilified and destroyed even in their own home lands. And America is still being built, and its interests are still being served, by Filipinos at the expense of their own continued destruction.

My American family, the Philippines's very Americanized climate today continues to propagate White, Western, American ideals to replace brown, indigenous, Filipino worldviews and cultures. This is supported by recent research that my brother Kevin and I conducted, which showed that 96 percent of Filipino immigrants in the United States experienced Filipino cultural denigration and American idealization while they were still living in the Philippines. Indeed, as noted American journalist and historian Stanley Karnow stated, ". . . in no place is the (American) imperial legacy more alive than in Manila, where America's presence is almost as dynamic now as it was during the days of U.S. rule."

About four years ago, when we took our first family trip to the Philippines, I was troubled—but not surprised—to see an abundance of skin-whitening products and clinics in Metro Manila, evidence that the masses have accepted the notion that the Filipino body is not as attractive as the White body. I also noticed how people admired all of you and your lighter skin tones, English proficiency, and American accents, automatically associating you with beauty and desirability.

During the same family trip, I also saw the continued discrimination against, and low regard of, non-Christian, non-urban, and non-Westernized Filipinos, sending the message to the masses that the more Western you look, think, and behave, the better off and more accepted you will be.

My ancestors' colonial history, my homeland's neo-colonial and highly Americanized modern reality, and the resulting widespread colonial mentality among my Peoples is why the "voluntary immigrant" or "voluntary minority" narrative—wherein individuals supposedly "choose" to leave for better opportunities in the United States, and that this "choice" is not forced by American society or people—is not and has never been completely accurate for Filipinos. America's colonization of the Philippines and the resulting Americanization and U.S. dependence of Philippine culture, standards, worldview, and economy, have created a context wherein it is almost inevitable for most Filipinos to cultur-ally and economically struggle. Such a postcolonial context also makes it so that, in order for Filipinos to rise from such hardships, they need to become as Americanized as possible. And what better way there is to Americanize than to be in America—or so goes the message that the Filipino masses receive. So people like me, your Lolo, your Uncle Bonz, your uncle Pum's wife and her family, and millions of others end up crossing the Pacific Ocean—even making it all the way up to Alaska—in search of what we were told was "better." Therefore, the large numbers of Filipinos com-ing into the United States—and overstaying in the United States—is not surprising, because many Filipinos already have a grandiose perception of America and a deteriorat-ed view of the Philippines, perceptions that are shaped by colonialism and a highly Americanized postcolonial climate. As political scientist Rodriguez stated,

> Colonialism has fostered a perception that... the U.S. is... a highly sophisticated society... adults dream of going to the U.S. as if longing to be reunited with a long-lost parent... children dream of becoming Americans... (and) finally be able to live in Disney's Kingdom... For many Filipinos, coming to America means the fulfillment of a lifelong dream.

Thus, Jose Antonio and millions of other Filipinos were born in a context wherein people saw America as a very viable and attractive option for social mobility—perhaps the only option—in order to escape the perceived hopelessness in the Philippines. And this is largely due to what America did, and is still doing, to the Philippines.

My American family, I think I understand the context Jose Antonio grew up in, at least a little bit, because I too grew up in the same context. It is a context wherein the legacy of Western colonialism and white supremacy is so strong, that it has become commonplace for brown-skinned Filipinos to desire lighter skin tones. It has become common behavior for brown-skinned, tropical islanders to avoid the sun—which is out most of the day every day all year round—so that they won't get too dark. It has become an accepted attitude to regard light skin as an indicator of beauty and desirability, and to regard dark skin as a sign of ugliness, undesirability, and inferiority. It has become accepted behavior to use skin-whitening creams, lotions, soaps, and even tablets; it is a place where skin-whitening clinics are abundant.

It is a context wherein anti-Black or anti-dark skin attitudes are not only common, but even accepted and encouraged. It is a context wherein the Aeta people—one of the Philippines's Indigenous Peoples who have black skin and curly hair—continued to be marginalized and discriminated against by dominant Filipino ethnic groups like the Tagalogs and Kapampangans who regard Aetas—and other fellow Indigenous Peoples—as uncivilized, uneducated savages. It is a context wherein parents and elders discourage their children, relatives, and friends from being romantically involved with or marrying Black or dark-skinned people. It is a context wherein marrying a White person—especially if American—means marrying up and is considered an accomplishment.

It is also a context where it has become an accepted attitude to regard English fluency as an indicator of intelligence, and to regard those who cannot speak English as lower class and stupid. It is a context wherein the official language used for school instruction is English, and English proficiency is regarded as a ticket to social mobility. It is a context wherein everything that was "Made in the USA" is valued and associated with better quality, while anything "Local" or "Made in the Philippines" is regarded as cheap, of poor quality, and only for the poor. I grew up in a context where anything Western or White, which has been equated with America, is associated with superiority, while anything Filipino is associated with inferiority.

And I bought into it. I succumbed to it. I absorbed it. It was all around me. It was like air, and I had no choice but to breathe it. I thought that's just how the world was. I thought hating my brown skin was normal, that wanting to look lighter-skinned and using skin-whitening products was normal. I thought staying away from the sun was normal. I thought I had to learn accent-free English to be successful in life. I thought Black people and other dark-skinned people were criminals, ugly, dumb, and dangerous. I didn't want to associate with such people. I thought Filipinos who weren't Westernized or Americanized, were backward, stupid, lower class. I didn't want to be associated with such Filipinos.

I lost my kapwa—my indigenous core value. It means fellow being. It is the essence of Filipino personhood, of being human. In kapwa, we are all on the same level, we are all equal, and we are all connected. Kapwa means shared inner self; it is how one exists in the other, and how the other exists in one.

My American family, I lost my kapwa because I learned to draw lines between me and my fellow beings. I succumbed to the imposed ways of separating myself from other people; they're too brown, too un-American, too uneducated, too rural, too indigenous, too Filipino. I internalized the oppression of my own culture. I internalized the oppression of my own Peoples.

So I dreamed of coming to the "USA"—like millions of Filipinos—because the USA has become our ideal, our measure of "success." Similar to how I separated myself from other Filipinos, I wanted to separate myself from the Philippines. I wanted to be associated with what I considered to be superior. I wanted to be in Disneyland, in Universal Studios, in Hollywood, in New York City.

But as disturbing as this may already seem, I need you to understand that this wasn't just my dream. This was also the dream of my parents, your Lolo and your Lola, because they also internalized the oppression and inferiorization of the Filipino culture and body. And this was also the dream of their parents, as they were also products of a colonized society wherein the systems and institutions propagated the notion of American superiority and Filipino inferiority. They, too, had their sense of kapwa damaged. They, too, were victims of colonialism, of cultural inferiorization, of cultural genocide.

My American family, oppression, colonialism, and colonial mentality are huge and complicated, and its effects are widespread. So my internalized oppression isn't unique. Jose Antonio's experiences and circumstances are not unique. The Filipino immigrant experience is not unique. There are millions of other immigrants in the United States, and they too are from countries that have been colonized, militarized, or significantly influenced by the United States in one way or another. United States colonialism and other forms of American cultural, military, or economic imposition—both historically and contemporarily—on various countries throughout the world need to be acknowledged and incorporated into how we think about the immigration issue, so that we can more completely understand immigrants' realities and experiences.

Just as the case for the millions of Filipino immigrants for whom American colonialism plays an important factor, the Latino, African, other Asian, and now even Middle

Eastern and Eastern European immigration and refugee experiences also need to be framed and understood in terms of United States colonialism and United States foreign policies. For instance, it is not a coincidence that the majority of the border children are coming from Honduras, Guatemala, and El Salvador—countries that the United States was involved in during the Contra wars, which led to the civil wars, economic instability, poverty, and extreme violence in these countries that are now being cited as the main reasons why children are seeking refuge in the United States. The United States has, at the very least, significantly contributed to the hopelessness that is currently being felt by many people in these Central American countries.

So you have to look at yourselves, too. And by "you" and "yourselves" I mean you and the millions of others who are privileged to be born in the United States or born with United States citizenship automatically secured. We need those of you who are native born to understand that people do not just wake up one day all of a sudden wanting to leave their home countries—everything and everyone they know, love, and are familiar with—and move into the United States. Immigrants and refugees and asylees are not genetically programmed to want to risk their lives—and those of their loved ones—just to cross America's borders. There is no such thing as an inborn "I gotta get to America even if it's a very dangerous journey that means leaving everything I love behind" instinct.

So my American family, I hope now you understand this about your immigrant father, about your immigrant husband. I am here, because America forced its way into my indigenous homelands. I am here, because America exploited, raped, and ravaged my indigenous homelands. I am here, because America destroyed my worldview and made me forget my ways of doing things, ways that allowed my ancestors to survive and thrive in our indigenous homelands for generations. I am here, because America forced me to believe that the American ways of doing things—that the American ways of seeing the world—are better. I am here, because America miseducated me and my Peoples. I am here, because America made me adopt American values and ideals at the expense of denigrating my indigenous values and ideals. I am here, because America made me hate myself, my Peoples, my culture, my body.

As Jose Antonio is fond of saying: "I am here, because America was there."

And now maybe you, as native-born Americans and as Indigenous Peoples of these lands, can help broaden other Americans' conceptualization of the immigration and refugee experiences of historically colonized or "American-influenced" Peoples. Maybe you can stand with our immigrant brothers and sisters—as you have stood with me—and help make other Americans consider how United States foreign interventions and impositions may have damaged other countries and influenced peoples' perceptions of and consequent movement to the United States.

Perhaps you can help convince other Americans that, with the "immigration problem," we need to look at the historical and contemporary contexts. Maybe you can make people consider the possibility that the United States brought this "immigration problem" unto itself. That

Americans also need to look at themselves and their policies as contributing to this problem. Even further, perhaps the solutions to this problem need to go beyond simply blaming and punishing the victims of such colonizing, imperialistic, and oppressive policies. Then, once we have looked at all the major players—or, dare I say culprits—perhaps a truly "comprehensive immigration solution" can be achieved.

My American family, as native-born Americans, you have more powers and privileges than others to help make this happen. I hope you are aware of this privilege. I hope you use this privilege. I hope you share this privilege. I hope you risk this privilege.

II. MY LOVE

Imperialism leaves behind germs of rot which we must clinically detect and remove from our land but from our minds as well.

—Frantz Fanon,
Wretched of the Earth,
(1965)

Kalayaan's drawing of her mom and dad on Valentine's Day 2017.

March 21, 2016

My Love,

I clearly remember when I first saw you at Eben Hopson Middle School in Barrow, Alaska.

I immediately noticed your brown hair, your light skin, your perfect English, your American accent, and your Tweety Bird T-shirt. You were the All-American girl I've been seeing in those teenager television shows I was using to teach myself to become more Americanized, to assimilate, to become White. You were Brenda Walsh from *Beverly Hills, 90210*. You were Winnie Cooper from *The Wonder Years*. You were Topanga Lawrence from *Boy Meets World*. You were Kelly Kapowski from *Saved by the Bell*.

Your first name is the quintessential American female name, and your last name reflects your Swiss-German heritage. You are European American. You are perfect; I was infatuated.

I remember when we started going out, and how incredibly lucky I felt to be with such a fair, White American girl. I remember showing my family and friends in the Philippines your photos—our photos as we spent time hanging out around the school, during basketball trips, and riding around town in the bus—and feeling extremely proud of how White and American you are.

I remember when we visited the Philippines together, traveling around my homeland together, and in many ways I remember showing you off to my Peoples like you were a trophy. And I also remember feeling how much my Filipino family and friends—how every Filipino we encountered—admired you because of your White American-ness. And by extension, I felt that they were seeing me as White American too. By extension, I felt their admiration of me—of my American-ness—too.

And it felt good.

But perhaps more important—and even more satisfying—than the admiration of my fellow Filipinos was the acceptance I felt, perhaps naively, from Americans because you went out with me. I felt American because of your acceptance. I felt like I belonged; that I was now one of you. I felt accomplished.

And I fell in love—deeply in love—with the thought that you and I would be together forever, that you and I would be married and have children together. I loved the thought of being forever bound to you—my All-American White girl—and having White, mestiza or mestizo, light-skinned American children together. I fantasized about such a life with you, as you were going to bring me even closer and more fully toward being in the mainstream, to being White, to being American. You and our light-skinned, English-speaking, Filipino accent-free American children were going to be the ultimate victory of my colonial mentality.

But, damn, was I wrong! And I'm so glad to be wrong.

I found out that you are also Alaska Native—Koyukon Athabascan to be exact—indigenous to these lands. I found out that you are very proud of your indigenous heritage, and that you feel very strongly connected to your ancestors. It was the White American I was attracted to and what

I was looking for to help me get through my struggles in this life, to bring me up the social hierarchy and become a "success" in this world. But it was the indigenous person who rescued me from my rapid fall down the sad, empty, meaningless abyss of colonial mentality.

Over the twenty-two-plus years that we've known each other, you have taught me plenty.

You taught me about your culture, your heritage. You brought me to Ruby, Rampart, Tanana, and a few other villages on the Yukon River. You even made me kayak down the Yukon River—for hundreds of miles! You told me about your Peoples, and how they—like my ancestors—are also Peoples of the River. I learned about your grandparents and how they lived. You shared with me the story of how Setsoo Lillian was born a few months premature on a trapline in the middle of winter, hundreds of miles away from the nearest village, and how this was representative of how strong and resilient she was all throughout her long life. You also told me about how Setsoo Lorraine shot a giant brown bear lurking around her fish camp, because that's just what she does.

You exposed me to your Native core values, to Native humor, to Native beliefs and assumptions. You exposed me to different body languages, to different ways of communication, to different thought patterns. You exposed me to your culture's family roles, gender roles, and role expectations. You also exposed me to the stereotypes, biases, and prejudices that exist in your Native community.

You took me to meet Auntie Nora, and you made sure that I got to know her pretty well. We laughed and marveled together at the fact that she still rode her four-wheeler around the hills of Ruby at the age of ninety. We laughed and marveled together at the fact that, even after we have repeatedly told her that I am Filipino and even after I made garlicky chicken adobo in her house for her granddaughter's wedding, she still referred to me as "the Eskimo," simply because I lived in Barrow, but perhaps also because she has no idea what a "Filipino" is.

You took me berry picking, and showed me how so many Alaskan plants were used as foods and medicine by your ancestors. You showed me moose, you showed me salmon. You fed me moose, and you fed me salmon. And, oh my goodness, the moose and the salmon!

You showed me how resilient and strong and fierce your Peoples are. You showed me how families and communities come together, and share with each other, and help each other, and step up to fulfill multiple roles in the community when need arises. You taught me how this is essential for survival, especially in the harsh, unforgiving Alaskan landscape.

You taught me about your history, your Peoples' history. You shared the good parts, but also the painful parts.

You taught me about trauma. You taught me about historical trauma.

You taught me about how your People's lands were taken away. Through you and your network of Native Peoples, I learned how this country was built on murder, rape, lies, exploitation, stolen lands, and broken promises.

You taught me how your People's language and worldview was taken away. You don't even speak your indigenous language—Denaakk'e—anymore, because of the cultural annihilation brought on by American colonialism. You also told me how you're trying so hard to get as much of it back as you can.

Through you I learned about the atrocities committed at the Wrangell Institute Boarding School and other Native boarding schools, wherein Native children were emotionally, psychologically, physically, and sexually abused. I learned that their indigenous languages and cultures were literally beaten, whipped, washed, and spanked out of Native children. You taught me how cultural loss and cultural genocide affected your Peoples. You taught me how it has affected multiple generations.

I learned about the soul wound.

I learned how the soul wound has affected your parents, your siblings, you. I learned how the soul wound has wreaked havoc on Native communities throughout Alaska and throughout the country. I learned about how the soul wound leads to many of the symptoms we see among Native Peoples today, issues like alcoholism, drug abuse, crime, incarceration, poor school performance, domestic violence, sexual abuse, depression, and suicide.

And from these realizations, I began to draw some similarities between the experiences of your Peoples and the experiences of my Peoples. The historical colonialism and cultural loss that Filipinos experienced, the damaging or loss of kapwa—the Filipino soul wound, if you will—may also be contributing to low self-esteem, high rates of depression, smoking, alcohol use, and unhealthy diets that may lead to the higher risks for cancer, heart disease, hypertension,

stroke, liver disease, diabetes, unintentional injuries, HIV/
AIDS, and other sexually transmitted diseases that have
been found among Filipinos.

Through you and with you, I learned that people who
internalized the oppression they experienced are likely to
have their physiological organs age earlier and deplete faster,
and so people with internalized oppression tend to die soon-
er. So I learned that my internalization of the oppression
that I and my Peoples experienced—my colonial mentality—has a very real negative effect on my physical body.

My colonial mentality has been literally killing me.

And together, we learned that this wound among our
Peoples is passed on intergenerationally; that you and I inherited risks for all of these unwanted social, educational,
and health outcomes from our ancestors. So I learned how
our kids need to watch out for this too. I learned how our
kids are at risk for suffering from the effects and manifestations of the soul wound. I learned how our children
inherited risk factors from both me and you. And this just
makes me angry.

It's so unfair—and so damn fucked-up—how being
Native and Filipino have become risk factors.

It is so infuriating to realize that our children are at
risk for a multitude of negative social, economic, education,
and health outcomes simply because of who they are. It is
so enraging to know that our heritage—something that we
should be proud of—has instead become a marker for so
many undesirables.

But see, the key term there is *become*. Being Native
or Filipino or brown is not naturally a bad thing. Being
Native or Filipino or brown is not inherently a risk factor.

It has "become" that way, because of what our society has attached to such characteristics. It has "become" that way because of the histories of colonialism, of cultural genocide, of racial oppression that our Peoples experienced and are still experiencing. It has "become" that way because of the denigrating and dehumanizing stereotypes that our Peoples have been and are still subjected to. Being Native or Filipino or brown has *become* a risk factor because of how our society perceives and treats people who are like us.

But I didn't always know this, my love. I didn't always believe this.

✦ ✦ ✦

I love you. I learned a lot from you, and I learned a lot with you. But as you already know, there are still some things that I learned independently of you that I am sure you understand and sympathize with, but can never fully relate to and empathize with.

Similarly, I love Barrow because this is where I met you. But as you know, there are many other reasons why I love Barrow that you know about and understand, but will probably never completely relate to because they weren't part of your lived experience. And some of these other reasons why I love Barrow are experiences that challenged me, confused me, destroyed me, and made me. I love Barrow also because, although this is the place where I had nightmares, it is also the place where I began to wake up.

As you know, there was a time when I thought it was normal for me to be ashamed of and hate being Filipino and brown. Similarly, there was also a time when I bought into the stereotypes about Native Peoples, when I automatically assumed that they were alcoholics, dumb, slow, dirty, and inferior. Not only did I internalize the oppression my Peoples faced, I also internalized society's oppressive beliefs about Native Peoples. While growing up in Barrow, however, I began to see how my assumptions and stereotypes about Native Peoples were wrong.

Through my time going to school there, playing basketball there, and working there, I saw how generous and kind and supportive and welcoming many Inupiaq People are. Through Pum, I learned what true loyalty means. He was always all-in. Even if I was on the wrong side, he was with me without hesitation. I remember one night after partying and Pum, and one of our homegirls, and I were driving home, and a cop pulled us over for "swerving," even though all I was doing was avoiding potholes on the Barrow dirt roads. I was not sure exactly what his motivation was, but Pum began acting like a funny drunk even though he wasn't drunk. Pum asked the police silly questions about what it was like to be an officer, what kind of gun he carries, whether he likes his patrol car, and even if Pum could go inside and check out the patrol car! With his behaviors, he successfully distracted the police officer's attention from me—the driver—and intentionally brought it on to himself. He got in trouble that night, and lost privileges for many months. I, on the other hand, kept my spot on the basketball team.

This is just one example. Pum took the fall for me many times. He took the blame for me countless times. He got my back all the time. And all of these experiences with Pum began to chip away at my long-held and solidified stereotypes and prejudices about Native Peoples, about Peoples of Color, including myself.

And over the years I had many other realizations about Native Peoples through Pum. Through him and his family, I saw how ingenious and resilient and strong the Inupiaq people are. Through Pum, his family, and many of the Inupiaq families I have been privileged enough to get to know—the whalers, the hunters, the trappers, the educators, the healers, the culture bearers, the village leaders—I saw how much the Inupiaq people valued their worldview, their ways of doing things, their language, their culture.

It made me question why I don't have that. It made me ask myself why—instead of pride—I have feelings of shame and embarrassment toward my heritage. Was I just born that way? Are Filipinos just born to want to get rid of their brown skins? Are Filipinos born desiring to be White? Are Filipinos born feeling ashamed of their culture, and wanting to separate themselves from their heritage? Are these Filipino inferiorizing attitudes and beliefs natural?

I also saw in Barrow the struggles of our Inupiaq brothers and sisters. I saw, heard, and felt the discrimination they faced. For example, I saw how that cop looked at Pum and automatically assumed that he was just another drunk Native kid. I also remember, when I was working at the Alaska Commercial Company as a grocery stocker for my after-school job, a belligerent—perhaps drunk—White man made a scene at the store by yelling curse words and harassing customers. When my manager and store security attempted to calm him down, he saw me, my cousin, and an Inupiaq coworker and yelled: "Fucking Filipinos! You come here and take all the jobs! You and all you Native fucks always ruin shit!"

And so this, and many other similar experiences, reminded me of the hateful words and actions that have been hurled toward me and my Peoples. I became conscious of the discrimination that I faced, and the violent oppression that my ancestors faced. I realized that I was not born hating myself. I realized that Filipinos aren't born hating their culture and their heritage. These inferiorizing attitudes and behaviors were learned, and racial oppression through colonialism and continued racism—in both the Philippines and the United States—were the teachers. As feminist scholar Nilda Rimonte eloquently states:

> (Colonial mentality's)... most common form is victim-blaming that includes hypercriticism and self-bashing ∴ (but) "the Filipino penchant for self-denigration" ... has a historical origin that can be diced and sliced. No longer can it be ascribed simplistically and incorrectly... to "Pilipino kasi!"—implying a curse of mis-shapen genes, or dismissed as a dismaying character flaw. This penchant for self-bashing is rooted in a history of race-based systematic inferiorizing strategies... and its residual effects continue to resonate to this day.

And as pioneering psychologist Gordon Allport asks,

> What would happen if you heard it said over and over again that you were lazy, a simple child of nature... had inferior blood.....[your] natural self-love may, under the persistent blows of contempt, turn your spirit to cringing and self-hate.

My love, historical colonialism and contemporary oppression said it over and over again. Historical colonialism and contemporary oppression inferiorized and denigrated the Filipino culture and body over and over again. Through historical colonialism and contemporary oppression, we were dehumanized repeatedly enough that we now destroy and hate ourselves. My Peoples were damaged enough that we now separate and divide ourselves according to the standards that White, Western people have imposed on us. Historical colonialism and contemporary oppression have destroyed and taken away our kapwa.

And it was in Barrow that I began to understand this. And because kapwa is about seeing one's interconnectedness with other human beings or other Peoples, I began to see the connections between myself and the Inupiaq Peoples. Interestingly, I learned that Inupiaq—and other Alaska Native groups like the Yup'ik and your Peoples the Dene—means "Real People." And given that kapwa is the core of Filipino personhood—it is what makes a person a Filipino, a human, a Tao—it is quite remarkable that the start of my kapwa recovery was literally centered on connecting with other "Real Peoples."

So I love Barrow, because it was where I began to make connections between the Inupiaq and the Filipino experience, between the experiences of America's First Peoples and those of my ancestors. It was in Barrow when I began to learn about Indian Boarding Schools, about Alaska Native Boarding Schools, and the atrocities that happened in such places. It was in Barrow when I learned about how Natives were forced to assimilate and become White, just like what was done with my Peoples. It was in Barrow when I began to learn about the "Great Death" and the Aleut internment camp. It was in Barrow when I began to learn about the stereotypes and prejudices that Native Peoples are subjected to on a daily basis, similar to the denigration and marginalization that my Peoples face.

My love, it was in Barrow where I first saw you. And it was also in Barrow when I began to see.

After graduating from Barrow High School and moving on to the University of Alaska Anchorage, I became even more aware of how society sees me and my brown skin, how society hears me and my accented broken English, and how society feels about me hanging out with you—a beautiful White-passing woman.

Remember when—as college kids—you, your sister Lena, and I were driving through Canada? Remember what the border officer did? You and Lena didn't get any more than a look after he thumbed through your passports. But me, even though I wasn't driving at that time, I was asked to step out of the car after he carefully scrutinized my American passport. Remember when the border officer asked me if I've ever committed any crime? Remember when he said, "Are you sure?" after I said no? Remember when he further asked, "Are you sure, you haven't murdered anyone?"

I remember this vividly, because I felt so small, weak, harassed, belittled, vulnerable, and embarrassed as a brown-skinned immigrant man standing on the side of the road by international borders, being interrogated by authorities about being a potential criminal, in front of my girlfriend. It was traumatic. You knew it was wrong, and you knew it affected me. You knew it shook me.

Nevertheless, remember how I just "took it" and "brushed it off"?

These kinds of experiences are not rare though, as you know. For instance, do you remember that time when we used your mom's truck to drive from Fairbanks to Anchorage—I was driving—and we got pulled over by a state trooper? You noticed how worried I was, so you suggested that we switch places quickly, so that you would appear to be the driver, before the trooper got to us, so that he would have to deal with you instead of me. More than simply a nice gesture, that moment showed me that you not only understand my fears as a brown-skinned immigrant man, but that you also understand your privileged status as a White-passing woman. And you tried to use that privilege—to risk it even—to help me. That was cool.

That wasn't the only time we've used—or thought of using—your privilege to our advantage in one form or another. For example, whenever we need to get simple "favors," like getting better airplane seats or getting late fees waived or getting a refund for something we purchased, we always send you and never me. This is because we've learned together that whenever it is me that people see and hear, not only do we not get our simple "favors," I even get illogically harassed and inconvenienced. You've seen firsthand how differently people see me, regard me, and interact with me compared to how they treat you. For instance, you and I have had several conversations about how I seem to always get "randomly" selected for extra screenings at airports.

Speaking of airports, remember when Malakas was about two years old, and the three of us were visiting your family in Bozeman, Montana, but Malakas and I had to go back home to Anchorage a couple of days ahead of you? We all went to the Bozeman airport together, but it was just Malakas and I who went to the check-in counter, because we were the only ones traveling. Remember when I had to go back and get you, because you had to confirm to the lady at the counter that I am Malakas's father? On one hand, I'm glad they made sure that my child—or any child—is protected from being abducted. On the other hand, however, I wonder if they ask every adult traveling with a child that same question, and if they make every adult traveling with a child to go back and get consent and confirmation from the other parent. And I wonder if all the other parent has to do to prove and make such confirmation is to say "yes."

I wonder if it was the other way around—if you were traveling with Malakas—if doubts about you being his mother would even be raised. I wonder if they would ask you to get the father—me—to give consent and confirmation. And I wonder if all I'd have to do to prove that Malakas was my child and alleviate people's doubts would be to say, "Yes, I am his father and I give consent." I wonder. I doubt.

Shit, you were even able to travel internationally with our daughter without me; not one person questioned you, asked for documents attesting that you were her mother, and demanded that you show proof that I consented to let you take our daughter to another country! My love, you and I—together—have seen how differently the world treats you and me. You and I—together—have felt how differently the world treats White folks and Peoples of Color. You and I—together—have been appalled, saddened, and angered by the daily insults and injustices that are faced by darker-skinned immigrant people, like me.

But, we both know these are common experiences. We both know oppression is redundant. And over the course of my life I've learned to adapt to this, to develop "coping skills" or "defense mechanisms" to protect myself. I'm not saying that how I've learned to deal with this is beneficial, adaptive, or constructive. I'm not saying that at all. It's just that such things happen so often that I have no choice but to naturally develop a response, and the best response for me is to simply survive.

You already know how much I panic and tense up whenever I see police cars while I'm driving. You've already seen—many times—how my stress response goes up ten notches whenever I get pulled over and cops ask me questions and check out my documents. That's the fight or flight response, and I always choose flight in these cases because I know I can never win this battle. So in such situations, I will probably always just "take it" and "brush it off."

I'm sure you have also noticed how I always go to extra lengths to make sure I am not breaking even the most trivial of laws. For example, you seem to always tease me for still using my turn signals even though it is just to turn into our own driveway. But beyond this, have you noticed how careful, cautious, or paranoid I tend to be overall? I guess you can look at this as an attempt to prevent situations wherein I would have something to "take" and "brush off." It's self-protective; it's self-preservation. But, as you know, shit still happens to me despite how extra-vigilant I am.

Even good people and institutions who I thought knew me and thought I could trust, sometimes still end up throwing shit at me for me to "take" and "brush off." And perhaps especially in such situations, when people have some "power" over me because of the relationship we have, I am sure you've noticed how passive—maybe even goofy—I get. For instance, do you remember a few years ago when my alma mater and employer—the University of Alaska Anchorage—used my smiling brown face on flyers to promote their Aviation Administration program even though I have nothing to do with that program at all? It was a blatant case of tokenism, wherein I was simply regarded as a random brown person, despite the fact that I have been affiliated with the university for a combined eighteen years as a student, alumni, and professor, despite the fact that I shared my story in several print, radio, and television advertisements promoting the university, and despite the fact that my story has never included aviation technology in any way. It was insulting, disappointing, and hurtful.

But remember how I just shrugged my shoulders and pretended to find it kind of funny?

My love, I'm sure you've noticed how I very rarely complain or "stand up" for myself, and how nonconfrontational I am in general. For example, I know you've noticed how I often just let it go when I don't get the food that I ordered and paid for; or when someone cuts in front of me in line; or when all the other (White) men get referred to as "sir," but when it comes to me I'm a "buddy"; or when my professor mistakes me for one of her other Filipino students who is significantly shorter and less heavy and who, unlike me, has no facial hair. Do you remember all the conversations we've had about depending on other people to help me? Do you remember how difficult it was for you to convince me to ask others for help, to trust people? And do you ever get annoyed with the fact that I never want to be late for anything, that I'd rather get places early and wait for the person I am supposed to meet, or wait until I board the plane, or wait forever for whatever? This is because I know no one would do me any favors, wait for me, or give me extra chances. This is because I don't want to inconvenience anyone. And do you ever get annoyed with the fact that I never want to inconvenience anyone?

When we eat out, I know you have noticed how I always tip well, even when—sometimes *especially when*—the server was rude to me. As I've shared with you before, this is because I don't want others to think that people like me are cheap; because I don't want others to think that people like me are poor; because I don't want to live up to stereotypes that others may have about people like me; because I want to teach people that I have money, that I tip well, so that the next person who looks like me who comes into the same restaurant can hopefully be treated better.

But have you noticed how I never fill out those satisfaction surveys to call out rude servers, or racist servers, or bigoted servers? Do you see how I never complain to their supervisors? Have you noticed that I don't complain in general? My love, I'm sure you've noticed how I frequently just "take it" and "brush it off." Sometimes, you may even have seen me laugh it off.

This is because I don't want to subject myself to any more possible discrimination, to possible stereotype-confirmation, to any more potential rejection and ridicule, to possible burdens that can add to the already-heavy allostatic load I am carrying. I don't want to be subjected to any more mental, psychological, emotional, spiritual, and even physical pain.

I just want to move on already. I just want to get out of there. I just want to get home. I just want to live. I just want to survive.

So I just "take it" and "brush it off."

My love, it's exhausting! You see, whenever I experience racism, my thoughts and emotions go through the same type of processes, steps, and struggles—the same questions—time and time again. And these internal struggles are mentally, psychologically, emotionally, and physically taxing—just like the experience of racism itself.

One of the first questions that comes to mind in such instances is, "Am I just being overly sensitive?"

Everyone who has experienced racism has probably asked themselves this question; a question that distrusts our reality and doubts our sanity. I know you've experienced this too. It is even possible that you—as a White-passing Person of Color—have experienced more subtle or covert racism because other people may not see you as a Person of Color, and so they think it is "safe" to express racist statements and behaviors in your presence. So I'm sure you've asked yourself this question many times. This is when we try to determine if the comment or behavior we encountered was motivated by some type of bias or if it was driven by stereotypes about our race, ethnicity, or culture. Today's kind of racism is often not so obvious and clear-cut and may often be interpreted as a joke or as unintentional behavior that should just be let go and not be taken seriously.

Interpreting experiences of racism in such dismissive and minimizing ways, however, can lead us to self-blame: Like, "Oh, it's my fault, I'm just being too paranoid and oversensitive." Have you ever thought this? This line of reasoning is dangerous because it might lead us to change ourselves, to learn to tolerate oppression, instead of the perpetrators and systems of oppression being the ones to be confronted and changed. Thus, succumbing to the "I'm just being too paranoid and oversensitive" narrative may inadvertently reinforce racism because it is left unchallenged.

And given the work that I do, I am aware that I need to resist internalizing the oppression that I experience. I know oppression exists, and so I tend to hold a level of healthy paranoia and usually favor my own reality to avoid blaming myself for the racism I face. As noted psychologist Dr. Derald Wing Sue stated, although "power is often correlated with economic and military might... 'true' power resides in the ability to define reality." So perhaps, because of my awareness of oppression, I have been able to take this "true power" to protect myself.

So I get this far, my love, but what I do—or not do—after I exercise my power to define reality is where things get exponentially more difficult. Being conscious or aware is one thing. But being strong and brave enough to turn consciousness, awareness, or wakefulness into action is something else. Sure, I am now able to see, but whether or not I do something about what I see—and how I do it—is what I am struggling with right now. This is where I get stuck, my love. This is where I feel helpless and depressed. This is where my weakness, my cowardice—my lack of mental, emotional, and spiritual strength—take over.

You see, after I determine that I did just experience racism, I ask myself if I should just let it go—should I just "take it" and "brush it off"? Or should I speak up and educate and resist? Should I flight or should I fight?

I understand that calling out and standing up to instances of racism are small but powerful ways in which marginalized peoples can reclaim some power and have their realities heard and validated. I also understand that no one is educated and informed by simply escaping the situation, by simply "taking it" and "brushing it off," by doing nothing—which again leaves racism unchallenged—and so not doing anything may inadvertently reinforce racism as well. Besides, perpetrators of racism are the ones we need to confront and educate, so perhaps such experiences of racism are opportunities to not just "preach to the choir." Even further, I sometimes even think about how Peoples of Color like us need a voice and we need a different perspective "on the table," so perhaps this is an opportunity to be heard.

But as I have already told you, I very rarely speak up, resist, or educate because—in real-life racism encounters—such options of confrontation are easier said than done. As you know, in real-life racism encounters, the options of speaking out, resisting, or educating have very real, painful, traumatic, and dangerous consequences. Even for a White-passing Person of Color like you, instances of racism probably force you to regularly struggle with "outing" yourself as a Person of Color, speaking up, resisting, and educating folks. Perhaps you also often find yourself wanting to simply survive as well, and so maybe there are many times when you just "take it" and "brush it off." In fact, there might even be a strong tendency to just ride the invisibility of your heritage and hide your "Person of Color-ness," to continually benefit from your White-passing privilege, and not risk losing that privilege.

Unlike you, I don't have the privilege to pass as White. I don't have that privilege to risk, to potentially give up and lose. My color, my heritage, my immigrant status, and my "not from here" identity are completely out and clearly visible for everyone to see. So to me racism, including the kind that intersects with xenophobia, is always literally "to my face," and is directly insulting and demeaning. So what is one to do when faced with such blatant attacks on one's characteristics?

Some might think that the "natural" response in such situations is to defend one's self, to fight for one's basic humanity and honor. But, my love, I have to resist this "natural" response, because I live in a society filled with institutions and systems that were built over many generations to benefit and protect racism and other forms of social group oppression. I have to resist the "natural" response, because there are very real dangers that come with defending myself and fighting back against racism in a racist society. In real-life racism encounters, choosing to go with confrontation is literally choosing to risk one's dignity, humanity, and life. In a racially oppressive society, it has become the case that the "natural" response is to survive.

So I often just "take it" and "brush it off."

And even in those rare instances when I do seriously entertain the option of speaking up and resisting and educating, I also automatically and simultaneously ask myself if I have that responsibility to speak up, to represent, to defend myself and my Peoples? And why? Why can't I just simply "take it" and "brush it off"—the option that requires the least effort and the one that has the most immediate self-protective function?

As a person who has some understanding of racism, and as someone who my community has helped for many years to become educated, gain some credibility, and develop into some form of a "community leader," my answer to the question of obligation and responsibility is always "Yes!" But my survival instinct almost always wins out, my love, as I typically convince myself that I do not have to speak up with thoughts such as: "It's not a good idea to rock the boat. Besides, speaking up probably won't even change anything," and "It's not fair to be burdened with having to do the explaining all the time," and "This literally hurts my heart, it can't be good for my well-being. I am sucked dry, so I am done speaking up."

I, and most likely many other Peoples of Color, constantly feel pressured to represent, defend, and speak up, and oftentimes I feel exhausted—even hopeless—because I see the need to confront and resist again and again and again when it seems that doing so is not changing anything. Do you ever feel like this too?

And then, if I am really seriously considering speaking up and resisting and educating, I am also further burdened with the necessity to craft my confrontation in a certain way. I need to do it nicely, politely, and nonthreateningly, in order to be heard and be effective. But this is a very daunting, almost impossible task.

As you know, racism can linger and damage one's mind and especially one's heart, which is why it is almost impossible to talk about racism without one's heart. It is an almost impossible task to call out and talk about racism—even when I had a chance to organize my thoughts, even when I remind myself to keep my composure, and even when I start off speaking calmly—without my emotions coming out at some point.

As you know, when I talk about racism, I am not simply talking about an experience that I read about in some book or journal article. I am not just talking about a hypothetical scenario or a story that I saw in a movie. When I talk about racism, I am talking about my lived experiences, and my ancestors' lived experiences. This is real to us! So of course there are emotions—and painful ones—that will influence how I talk about this! Expressing emotions when I talk about racism doesn't make me any less credible, nor does it make my experiences less real.

But, my love, I am constantly reminded by this society that it does. I have been conditioned to believe that I can be more effective if I am more "respectful" or "professional," so that I am able to be more "palatable" to the audience I am trying to reach. So even during what is supposed to be an empowering moment for me—if I am even strong enough to choose to speak up, resist, or educate—I am reminded that I still need to cater to my oppressors, make sure that I do not offend my oppressors, and behave in ways that my oppressors deem "acceptable."

So yeah, this is why most of the time I just "take it" and "brush it off." It's because it's just easier. It's just the least painful. It's because I just want to survive. And so I just let it go.

Does this mean I am simply tolerating it? Does it mean I may be propagating it? Does my silence mean I am complicit to it? Does this mean that I failed my community? Did I fail myself? Did I fail to represent and defend my Peoples? Did I fail you? Am I weak? Am I a coward? Am I a sell-out?

Very recently, I have learned that, according to research, these internal struggles are common and can negatively affect a person's well-being. I also learned that not being able to speak out against racism, especially when one really wants to, can lead to lower self-esteem, feeling fake or feeling like a sell-out, loss of integrity, feeling that one let down one's social group, self-anger, and self-blame.

So shit. This is another kind of a catch-22 situation, wherein if I do something then I might be hurting myself. But if I don't do anything, I am still hurting myself.

So, is me just "taking it" and "brushing it off" and not speaking out against the injustices and mistreatments I experience a sign that I am accepting the inferiority that is imposed on and assumed about me? Does this mean that, despite all of my awareness and "critical consciousness" and "ethnic pride," I still struggle with internalized oppression? Despite all of my education and decolonization and kapwa recovery and indigenization, does my continued passivity and feelings of hopelessness mean that I still struggle with a colonial mentality?

Have I so deeply internalized the oppression that I experienced that it now exists and operates and affects me, even when I don't want it to or even when I purposefully try my best to stop it?

Unfortunately, I think yes. There is a very deep and solidified sense of inferiority, weakness, powerlessness, vulnerability, irrelevance, and invisibility that I have internalized as a brown-skinned, immigrant, colonized, and forgotten Person of Color. And I am afraid that, no matter how hard I try, I will probably never unlearn it.

It looks like I've taken too much damage, and I cannot simply just "brush it off."

My love, I'm afraid the damage is permanent.

III. MY SONS

There is nothing uniquely evil in these destroyers or even in this moment. The destroyers are merely men (and women) enforcing the whims of our country, correctly interpreting its heritage and legacy. It is hard to face this. But all our phrasing—race relations, racial chasm, racial justice, racial profiling, white privilege, even white supremacy—serves to obscure that racism is a visceral experience, that it dislodges brains, blocks airways, rips muscles, extracts organs, cracks bones, breaks teeth. You must always remember that the sociology, the history, the economics, the graphs, the charts, the regressions all land, with great violence, upon the body.

—Ta-Nehisi Coates,
Between the World and Me,
(2015)

Malakas looking out to the water and the mountains on July 4, 2016.

March 27, 2016

My Sons,

The two of you drive me nuts!

You make me so frustrated, because you don't pay attention. I get so exasperated because you don't listen. You don't listen the first time I ask you to do something. You don't listen when I am trying to get your attention. You don't listen when I am giving you instructions. You don't listen when I am lecturing you about not listening.

Sometimes I get so irritated that I even raise my voice and end up yelling at you. Sometimes I may even seem mean, nasty, intimidating, and scary to you. Because, why do you always wait until I repeat myself over and over and over again and get to the point where I end up yelling at you before you finally pay attention, before you finally listen? For real.

But despite these occasional outbursts, I hope you don't become scared of me. I hope you don't misinterpret my frustration, my yelling, and my stern, firm ways of communicating as mean-spirited or ill-intentioned. I hope you don't see me as unnecessarily harsh, unsympathetic, strict, or demanding. I am deeply sorry for all the times that I get carried away. And I promise to do a better job of reminding myself that you are still children, that I need to be patient, and that sometimes I just need to let you be.

I love you Malakas. I love you Kaluguran. I will never ever do anything to hurt you.

It's just that my own emotions, insecurities, anxieties, and fears get the better of me sometimes. It's not my intention to get angry at you. Actually, I am never angry at you, and my outbursts are never driven by any sort of anger or animosity toward you. Instead, I need the two of you to understand that my seemingly cruel, insensitive, and strict ways are driven by my learned resentment and bitterness—and even learned helplessness—toward our world, and by my worries about you living in this world.

You see, even though I understand that you are still children and that perhaps I should be more lenient, give you lots of chances, and just let you two be children, I also know that you are Native children, that you are Filipino children. I also know that you are Native boys, that you are Filipino boys, living in this world. And I am afraid for you, for how you are going to thrive—or even just survive—in this world.

Malakas and Kaluguran—please pay attention. Please listen.

You need to understand that you are products of both your parents' colonized histories, by your ancestors' colonized histories, and recognize how your lives in this world are going to be influenced by such colonized histories. You need to understand that although your teachers and your textbooks and your friends and your politicians and other "authority figures" may tell you that colonialism happened a long time ago and that it's been long over, you need to resist such lies and see how the legacies of colonialism are still around today, and therefore, still significantly influence your lives today.

You need to know that the legacies of colonialism can still hurt you—mentally, emotionally, spiritually, and physically—and therefore potentially lead to your suffering and death.

Your ancestors were victims and survivors of cultural genocide. They were dehumanized and were taught to hate themselves. Their ways were demonized and were stripped away. Your ancestors were traumatized, yet their pains, grief, and misery were minimized and never acknowledged. And many of them had to do what they had to do to survive.

Many of them had no choice but to stop speaking their indigenous language and replace it with English. Some were forced to change their mannerism to adapt Western ways of interactions. They had to replace their indigenous beliefs and worldviews with what was portrayed as more civilized and enlightened ways of knowing. Some had no choice but to keep quiet and accept the denigration, mistreatment, and injustice they were subjected to. Many of them had no choice but to leave their homelands—everything they are familiar with and love—just so they and their families can survive. They were forced to dress, act, think, and believe like the colonizers, perhaps even adopting the colonizers' prejudices as their own. And so some of them hated their own Peoples, not realizing that they were also essentially hating themselves.

Many of them directed their anger and frustrations toward those who they perceived as less threatening—their children, their partners, themselves. And so many of them ended up inflicting violence on their own families, on their own loved ones. Some of your ancestors were forced to encourage their children to learn the Western, American ways so their children wouldn't suffer the same maltreatments and discrimination as they did. Some even taught their children to suppress the indigenous ways, to hide their heritage, because of the shame and stigma that has been attached to their cultures and bodies. And so many eventually hated themselves and others like them. Many of your ancestors felt helpless and hopeless. Many were forced to turn to alcohol, drugs, and other self-destructive vices to grieve for the losses, to mourn for their ancestors, to soothe their self-loathing, to numb the pains. And many were driven to end the pains, permanently.

And these pains and anger and sorrows and attitudes and behaviors—as maladaptive as they may be—were unsurprising responses to the violence and trauma that your ancestors faced. It just makes sense that they developed such "defense mechanisms" and "coping strategies"—it's just what they had to do as they tried to survive. And through how they raised their children, and what their children are exposed to in the home and out in the community, it also just makes sense for these maladaptive survival responses to be passed on to later generations. They have been passed on to me and your mom, and now to you.

My sons, historical trauma has wounded your ancestors, and their wounds haven't yet healed. And you inherited such wounds along with their violent and painful consequences for our Peoples.

According to research, your colonized Native and Filipino pasts—and the trauma, cultural loss, and soul wounds that such ethnic and cultural oppression brought to our Peoples—contribute to a wide range of very worrisome and gloomy outcomes today.

For instance, research tells me that Native boys like the two of you are the most likely to abuse alcohol and become addicted to alcohol when you're older. Native boys like you are also the most likely to use marijuana. Because you're Native boys, research tells me to worry about you dropping out of school, being suspended from school, and not finishing high school. Native boys like you also seriously think about and plan a suicide attempt at a troublingly high rate. Research also tells me that Native boys like you also have the highest risks of dying because of suicide.

These grim statistics, and their links to intergenerational trauma, remind me of one of my homeboys. He's Native from the interior—just like the two of you. I didn't know much about his parents, but what I did know was that my homeboy didn't seem to have a stable family life. He seemed to just hop from one friend's house to another with curious regularity. He seemed so free, that he could do whatever he wanted, show up for school only if he wanted, stay out as late as he wanted, sleep wherever he wanted, hang out with whoever he wanted, drink whatever he wanted, and smoke whatever he wanted. Not unlike my situation at that time, it seemed that no one was supervising him, or caring about him. And he also seemed like he didn't care what happened to himself; it didn't seem like he cared much for his life.

Then one day, when I was in college, he called me, sobbing uncontrollably. He just found out that both of his parents had died. I eventually learned that they got into a heated argument, when past pains and hurts—between them and caused by others to them—were brought up. And things spiraled out of control. I heard that my homeboy's father shot his wife, then shot himself. My homeboy also told me that his four younger siblings—who are around the same age as you right now—witnessed the argument, the violence, the murder-suicide.

That messed up my homeboy pretty badly. He struggled even more with life, performed even more poorly in school, got into serious trouble with the law, got even deeper into drugs and alcohol, and also seriously considered suicide. And I am sure his younger siblings were traumatized and affected by everything too. I wonder how they are doing now.

So you see, I worry about you as Native children, because your ancestors' traumatic colonized history can still have very real, destructive, and lethal manifestations today. And in addition to my worries about you as Native children with regard to the intergenerational trauma and associated risk-factors you may have inherited from your ancestors, I also worry about you as children of a colonized Filipino man with internalized oppression.

I worry about you developing feelings of shame and self-doubt. I worry about you having self-hate because you're Filipino. So I am concerned about you becoming depressed, being bullied, and having low self-esteem, issues that research tells me Filipino boys like you are likely to experience. And these issues may lead to eating disorders and body dissatisfaction, as research tells me that Filipino boys like you are at higher risk for these problems compared to many of your peers from other ethnic groups. These issues, in turn, may lead to poorer health when you get older, as being overweight or obese, having diabetes, and developing hypertension and coronary heart disease are also found to be common among Filipinos—and are significant contributors to our deaths. As Filipino boys, research also tells me to expect you to smoke cigarettes, and relatedly, to worry about you dying of lung cancer.

As Filipino boys, the sense of insecurity, low self-esteem, cultural loss, self-hate, and identity confusions that are brought on by colonialism and contemporary oppression may also lead to various other concerns for you. Research says I also need to worry about you joining gangs, or getting involved in criminal activities like damaging other peoples' properties, or getting arrested as juveniles. Research also tells me that Filipino boys like you are most likely to be suspended from school, cut school, get low grades in school, experiment with or abuse alcohol and other drugs, and have problematic aggressive behaviors compared to other Asian groups like the Chinese and Koreans.

Look, I know that all of these research references may seem boring to you, and you may feel like they don't relate to you. So let me make them real, let me bring them to life. Please allow me tell you a short—depressingly short—story.

Remember how I moved to Barrow from the Philippines as a young teenager? The very first friend I made in Eben Hopson Middle School, during my very first day in an American school, was a mestizo Filipino boy—just like the two of you. He was cool, fashionable, popular. He showed me where my classes were, toured me around the school, and introduced me to several other kids—kids who

I would end up playing on the same basketball team with. Over the years, my mestizo Filipino friend started struggling in school. I started seeing less and less of him; in fact, I don't believe he ever finished high school. He got into trouble with the law several times, got into fights, and got into drugs. He got involved in gang activities, and became a low-level drug dealer. And just five years ago, my mestizo Filipino friend was shot dead in the streets of Anchorage.

His killer? Another Filipino friend of mine who I played basketball with. He was another Filipino friend who also struggled in school, also got into drugs, also became a low-level drug dealer, and also got into trouble with the law as a juvenile.

My sons, that's the tale of two Filipino boys—just like the two of you. One of them is dead now, and the other is in jail for eighty-five years.

So please pay attention. Please listen.

✦ ✦ ✦

These are just a few of the reasons why I worry about you as Native and Filipino boys. Your mom and I know way too many young Native and Filipino boys—people we went to school with, are friends with, and are related to—who have struggled in life, passed on tragically, or inflicted pain on others due to the intergenerational legacies of historical trauma or loss of kapwa. I wish I could depend on our world to help me—to help you—address the risk factors and lower the likelihood that any of these undesirable things will happen to you. I wish I could optimistically tell you that our world can help correct all the wrongs of the past, along with its many negative consequences. But I can't.

Instead, based on what I know about our history, about our ancestors' experiences, and what I myself have directly experienced, this world won't even acknowledge half the wrongs that were done in the past. Our world won't even believe that the past still has anything to do with all the social, educational, economic, and health issues our Peoples are struggling with now!

So, yeah, I wish I could depend on the world. But unfortunately, the world will probably just continue to mess the two of you up. Perhaps mess you up even more.

Historical trauma has wounded your ancestors, and their wounds haven't yet healed. And it seems to me that our modern world won't do anything to heal such wounds. Instead, our world will probably even continue to infect such wounds, perhaps make it even worse, whip you up some more and add even more wounds, or perhaps make such wounds even more lethal.

You see, even if intergenerational violence and hurt and trauma don't get you, this current, modern world will try. The two of you need to understand that it's not easy being a Filipino man in this world. It's not easy being a Native man in this world. Just as you are a product of your ancestors' traumatic colonized histories, you are also going to be a product of our contemporary society's perceptions and stereotypes about Filipinos and about Natives.

You will deal with emasculation. You will deal with "drunk native" jokes. You will experience the "lazy native" stereotype. People will ask you "Where are you really from?"

You will be seen as a perpetual foreigner even though you are truly indigenous to these lands. People will ask about your long hair; other kids will tease you about your long hair. You will be treated rudely like a second-class citizen, perhaps even third-class, because even within the Asian American community you will be discriminated against, marginalized, and neglected. Because you are Filipino, this country and many of its people will categorize you as Asian, but many others won't see you as such; instead they might consider Filipinos as "Pacific Islanders" or the "Latinos of Asia" or the "Brown Americans of Asia" or the "Black Asians." Some people will simply be confused by you and ask, "What are you?" as if you are an object. You will probably never deal with "good at math" stereotypes like other Asians, instead you might deal with "dumb native" or "naive villager" stereotypes. I am not sure you will experience the "model minority" stereotype like other Asians, instead you might deal with "gangster" or "thug" stereotypes—people assuming you are deviant, up to no good, or involved in criminal activity. People will denigrate your traditional foods, while others may exoticize it and refer to it as "authentic" and "ethnic." People will relegate your indigenous languages to a lower level than English, perhaps even completely dismiss them altogether.

My sons, you will learn that racism is still all around you. And for evidence, I will give local Alaskan examples so you don't think that racism is just an issue in other places but not in our awesomely diverse home; so that you realize that this is real, that it's close to you, and that it can—and probably will—happen to you.

First is individual-level modern-day racism, which is not as overt and a lot more subtle or hidden than the racism of the past. Today, because it is no longer as socially acceptable to be blatantly racist as in the past, interpersonal racism often comes out in social media where people are usually protected by anonymity—or at least there's some distance between people as they interact with each other. For example, our fellow Alaskans said things like these over the internet about Michael Brown—the young Black man who was killed in Ferguson, Missouri, a couple of years ago by a White police officer named Darren Wilson.

> *"Mike Brown's parents should be disappointed that their son was a thug, made poor choices, and got himself justifiably killed."*

> *"Good, the thug had it coming."*

> *"The piece of shit thug got what he deserved."*

> *"The Anchorage Police Department needs to hire Officer Darren Wilson now to clean up in Anchorage. There are too many Samoans and Filipinos around here now."*

> *"I too hate and fear the colored race, so bravo for the correct decision."*

In addition to using the term *thug* as a more socially acceptable term than the *N*-word when referring to Black People, or as a code word that assumes all Peoples of Color are deviant, many of our fellow Alaskans also described the protests following the nonindictment of Darren Wilson as "typical jungle mentality"—reflective of the long-held tradition of seeing Peoples of Color as less than human and as uncivilized savages who are comparable to wild animals.

Another example is what happened less than a year ago in a neighborhood that is just a few blocks from our house in Anchorage, when our refugee brothers' car was vandalized with threatening messages telling them that they are "Not Welcome Here" and that they should "Leave Alaska" and "Go Home." That sent a clear, threatening, and serious message to our refugee and immigrant brothers and sisters that there are still hateful people in our midst. It sent a threatening message to immigrants—like me, your Lola, your uncle Bonz, and many more of your relatives— that there are still people around us who don't like us here.

And what about the racist messages that our institutions send? For example, up until a few months ago, the tallest peak in North America was officially named "Mt. McKinley" instead of "Denali," which is what the indigenous Peoples of these lands—your Athabascan Peoples—called the mountain. This is despite many efforts over the years to reinstate the mountain's original, indigenous name. So for decades, our institutions resisted acknowledging the mountain's indigenous name and sent the message to Alaska's Native Peoples that a White man's name is more official, desired, recognized, and acceptable. This was a reminder to many of the painful period of colonialism and blatant racism, when Alaska Native Peoples' worldviews and cultures—especially their languages—were devalued, demonized, and forcefully replaced by what were portrayed as more civilized ways.

I should also remind you that William McKinley, the United States president whose name officially adorned the Great Mountain, also saw Filipinos as inferior, uneducated, and uncivilized Peoples. And so to honor someone who held racist and oppressive beliefs against non-Western or non-White Peoples—your Native and Filipino ancestors—in a state as culturally and ethnically diverse as Alaska is to continue—in an institutionalized manner—the colonialism and oppression of the past. With the "McKinley" name, our institutions were telling Alaska Native peoples that their names, languages, and cultures are still not as good or as "legitimate" as Western names, languages, and cultures. Our institutions were still telling people today that oppression of the past is okay, or at least, it's time we forget because oppression is now dead. By honoring a person who devalued and belittled your Peoples, our institutions were sending the message that not only is it okay to be racist, you might even be honored by having a mountain named after you.

And what about systemic racism, specifically in our justice system? A recent and local example of this is the Fairbanks Four, four Native men—but were boys at the time of their investigations, trials, and convictions—who were sentenced to thirty-three to seventy-seven years of jail time for a crime they did not commit. Four Native men who, because of the questionable and biased police investigation and problematic evidence, were eventually released from prison after eighteen years, but only with the promise that they would not sue the police, the prosecutors, the City of Fairbanks, and the State of Alaska for any wrongdoings!

And, my sons, this happened in Koyukon Athabascan lands, your indigenous lands!

And you know what else this case tells us about our system? It tells us that four Native men can be convicted of murdering a White person with little, weak, and highly dubious evidence, but four murder convictions cannot be done for the four White men who brutally murdered a Filipino man, even though the entire murder was clearly caught on camera. My sons, I saw Ferdinand Marquez—a fifty-year-old Filipino fisherman—in his coffin, his face hardly recognizable because of the extremely inhumane manner with which those four White men beat and mangled him. I also saw how much sorrow his sisters were experiencing when I accompanied them to see Ferdinand's body. Yet I really can't imagine how much pain they were feeling at that time, and I don't ever want to know. But I don't think their pain was reduced by the injustice they got from the system.

Unsurprisingly, this same system also showed us that a White woman who was texting while driving, hit an Alaska Native man, left him to die, lied to people by saying that she hit a stray dog, and tampered with evidence by deleting the text messages she sent during the hit and run, got only eighteen months of jail time. We also see a White teenage boy who took his father's Chevy Tahoe without permission, smoked marijuana while driving, texted on his phone while driving, ram into a car carrying an Alaska Native family—including two young children—consequently killing the mother, get only one year of jail time, with the possibility of early release.

This is how much our system values—or devalues—Native and Filipino lives.

And what about the extent to which we have normalized and accepted racism as part of our culture, the extent to which we give people a pass for racism—when we minimize racism? Well, we need not look any further than our lone state representative to the United States Congress. He has a long history of "missteps," including a highly publicized reference to Mexicans as "wetbacks," yet during last year's election, an overwhelming number of Alaskans still elected him to his twenty-second term. Of course, many of our Alaskan neighbors and friends also have plenty of other things to say about our Mexican and Latino brothers and sisters, given the recent immigration debates, but they're too many to include here.

So you see, racism is alive and well in our modern American society, from Florida where Trayvon Martin—another young Person of Color who was unjustifiably killed—all the way to Barrow, Alaska—where your uncle Pum was also unjustifiably gunned down.

And although we may oftentimes just "take it" and "brush it off," or maybe even "laugh it off," you need to understand that racism is never harmless. There are consistent research findings based on various racial groups such as Alaska Natives, Native Americans, Asian Americans, Latinos/as, Pacific Islanders, and African Americans showing that racism is related to lower self-esteem, self-doubt, self-hate, cultural loss, and social isolation, all of which are important risk factors for various other concerns that are commonly faced by these communities—by our Peoples—such as depression, suicide, alcohol and drug use, poor school performance, gang involvement, engagement in high-risk behaviors, crime involvement, and others.

In addition to how historical colonialism and contemporary racism may damage you and how you in turn may damage yourself, you also need to understand that past and modern-day oppression can lead you to hurt other people. My sons, historical colonialism and contemporary oppression have beaten you down and will continue to beat you down as Filipino and Native men. The past and current devaluation of your humanity may contribute to your sense of inferiority as Filipino and Native men, and you need to understand how such insecurities may lead you to lash out at those who remind you of your alleged worthlessness—those who you perceive to be less powerful than you. So you need to resist violence against other Native People. You need to resist violence against other Filipino People. You need to resist violence against women and children.

Indeed, research shows disturbingly high rates of intimate partner violence and child abuse among our communities, and in many of these cases the perpetrators of violence and abuse are men. And there is also the epidemic of sexual assault and abuse, a large percentage of which are committed by men against women and children. In our home state of Alaska, for example, the rate of reported sexual assault has continued to grow over the past fifty years—pretty much how long Alaska has been a state—to our current level of nearly three times the national average. And these are just the reported cases! The Rape, Abuse, and Incest National Network have estimated that at least 60 percent of all sexual assaults go unreported.

And don't ever think that people who are victimized by violence and abuse are "asking for it" or that they "deserve" it. It's not their fault. It's never their fault.

Never believe the victim-blaming narrative that is perpetuated by this society. How victims were behaving and what they were wearing and what they were drinking and what they were saying and whether or not they were walking alone in a dangerous neighborhood and whether or not the victim "has a past" and whether or not the victim has self-defense training does not matter. There is no clear consistency among intimate partner violence victims or sexual assault victims to suggest that the cause of their victimization resides with them. There is no common factor among the victims to legitimately conclude that they are to blame for their own victimization. Instead, in all intimate partner violence and sexual assault cases, the only common factor is that there is an attacker. And most of the time, the attacker is a man. And research suggests that sexual assault and rape and intimate partner violence is almost always driven by the desire—or need—of the perpetrator to maintain, obtain, or retain power and control.

My sons, please do not buy into this toxic type of masculinity. You are not entitled to have power or control over anyone. You do not have to dominate anyone to be a complete man, or to be a complete person, or to prove anything to anybody. You do not have to validate violence or show a potential to commit violence in order to be respected. Do not view women, LGBTQ people, and other Peoples of Color—human beings that this world will try to convince you to see as inferior—as inherently being less than you. My sons, it's completely okay to be afraid, to admit weakness, to be caring, soft, tender, and vulnerable. These do not make you less of a man; instead, they complete you as a human. You need to understand toxic masculinity and identify it when you see it so that you can protect yourself from acquiring it. Toxic masculinity is harmful not only in terms of how you see yourself as a person, but it is also deadly in terms of how you regard and interact with other people in this world.

My sons, as Native and Filipino males, I understand that this world has and will continue to try to emasculate you, challenge you, anger you, agitate you, and force you to react violently—especially toward those who this world prescribes as less powerful. The oppressive systems in this world will try to convince you that the source of your problems is the other oppressed groups in society instead of oppression itself. This is how racism intersects with sexism and other forms of social group oppression. I understand that for many generations now this world has taken so much of your power. But you must resist and always remember that exerting abuse and power over the marginalized and vulnerable—or anyone for that matter—does not make you more powerful. Please, my sons, don't try to reclaim your power this way.

Native People are not your enemy. Filipino People are not your enemy. Women and children are not your enemy. Other Peoples of Color and other marginalized folks are not your enemy. You need to always have a broad and more complete, and therefore more accurate, perspective as to what really has been driving the issues and concerns we are facing in our communities. You need to understand that factors beyond victims and beyond individuals—larger sociopolitical factors such as colonialism and racism along with its intersections with sexism and heterosexism—play important roles in our struggles. So you need to understand that we cannot just blame victims or blame individuals or make changes on the individual level, because the problems did not begin there and does not reside there. The problems are outside of us. The problems are the deeply seeded bigoted values, biases, prejudices, and conventions that drive and emanate from the systems and institutions that we operate under, permeating our environment and, consequently, seeping into us.

So my sons—my Native and Filipino sons—please pay attention, please listen.

I need you to understand that interpersonal, internalized, and institutional racism and its intersections with other forms of oppression—like sexism, misogyny, heterosexism or homophobia—is here and all around our modern world. I need you to know this, and I need you to believe this. You can't ignore it, pretend that it doesn't exist, or take comfort in the delusion that it doesn't affect you, me, your Peoples, or our community.

I hope you see the damages that racism and all forms of oppression that emanate from and intersect with it have had and still have on people, on families, and on communities. I hope you see the damages that racism and all forms of oppression have had and still have on our Peoples, our families, and our communities.

My sons, oppression in all its forms and intersections is not dead; oppression is deadly.

✦ ✦ ✦

Malakas, do you remember last week when you, Kaluguran, and I were getting ready to do our normal routine of reading books before going to bed? The conversation went something like this:

E.J.: Okay, it's time to read guys. Go get a book to read.

MALAKAS: What's your book about Dad? Huh, it looks like it's about someone in jail.

E.J.: Yup. It's about many people who are in jail.

MALAKAS: *The New Jim Crow*. That doesn't even make sense.

E.J.: That's because you don't know what Jim Crow is.

MALAKAS: Well, what is it?

E.J.: I'll tell you when you're older.

MALAKAS: Tell me now.

E.J.: Well, you know how we've talked about how darker-skinned people in our country are not treated right? Jim Crow is about a time in our country, a long time ago, when darker-skinned people had to use different swimming pools, different bathrooms, different schools, different water fountains, different restaurants, and other things.

MALAKAS: Oh. But this book says "NEW." So it still happens?

E.J.: Yes, the book is about how there are still some ways in life—in our world—today where things are still separate for darker-skinned people.

MALAKAS: So is the book about how some people go to jail even though they didn't do anything? Does that happen? Is that true?

E.J.: Yup. Yup. And yup.

MALAKAS: Can you read it to me?

E.J.: When you're older.

Well, to be honest, I have no idea what "older" means. Just a week ago I refused to talk to the two of you about racism, because I felt that this topic was still too heavy for an almost-seven-year-old and a three-year-old. Yet here I am just days later writing you this letter. Frankly, I am not sure what the appropriate age is to talk to you about certain issues and topics, including this one. Honestly, many times I am just guessing at this whole parenting thing.

But now that I've thought about it, I think your curiosity and interest in the subject matter is already a sign that I can begin to talk to you about this. Maybe. I guess. So here it is.

Do you remember that one movie night at home when you were watching *The Adventures of Huck Finn*? I remember you being deeply troubled by some scenes in the movie, and how you teared up about how Jim was treated by "the light-skinned people," as you referred to them. And as much as I study and talk about racism, I had no idea how to talk to you about it at that moment. I was so glad your mom was there to handle that situation.

With your mom's wisdom and grace, do you remember her guiding us to have a conversation about how there was a time when light-skinned people treated darker-skinned people badly and unfairly? And then you looked at me, and said, "Like you Dad? You have brown skin." I nodded, and you teared up again, then covered up your face to hide your sadness. Then, to make you feel better, do you remember when I said, "But that was a long time ago. The bad things that were done to darker-skinned people that you saw in this movie don't happen anymore. This is a story from a long, long time ago."? Do you remember me saying that?

Well, I kind of lied.

You see, even though it is true that the story of Huck Finn is from a long time ago, darker-skinned people are still being treated very badly and very unfairly today. Peoples who are not light-skinned—people who are not White—are still perceived by society as lesser, as bad people, as threatening people. So as you so impressively inferred during our brief exchange last week, *The New Jim Crow* is essentially about how Black and Brown people—darker-skinned people—are still treated badly and unfairly today.

And although discussions about racism in our country are typically limited to our Black brothers and sisters, and more recently to also include our Latina sisters and Latino brothers, you need to understand that racism also applies to you, because you are also "darker-skinned people." You are Filipino. You are Native. You are a Person of Color.

And as Persons of Color, especially as Native boys like you and Kaluguran, research tells me that you are facing many of the same bleak and unfair realities that are described in *The New Jim Crow*.

You see, similar to how many Americans—even police officers—seem to hold negative stereotypes about Black people, which then leads to discriminatory behaviors toward Black people, there is also research suggesting that many Americans hold deeply ingrained stereotypes about Native Peoples, too. For instance, research suggests that when Americans think of Natives, they also automatically think of "savage," "primitive," "dirty," and "lazy"—concepts that may lead to bad, unfair, or unjust behaviors toward Native Peoples. These automatic negative attitudes toward Native Peoples may contribute to the many issues they face with regard to the justice system today.

As an example, these automatic negative biases against Natives Peoples are probably parts of the reasons why police officers, investigators, and jury members were so quick to put blame on the Fairbanks Four back in 1997, despite the weak evidence against them. Indeed, commenting on the high numbers of Alaska Natives in the prison system back in 2003, when he was general counsel for the Tanana Chiefs Conference, Ethan Schutt stated: "I think it's easier to convict Native people than other defendants or ethnic groups. Police and prosecutors seem to be more vigorous in pursuing Native defendants, and jurors seem more willing to believe the authorities and disbelieve the defense when Native defendants are on trial."

And just like our Black brothers and sisters, Native Peoples also compose a troublingly and disproportionately high percentage of the prison population. Do you know that Native Peoples are incarcerated at a rate that is 38 percent higher than the national average? And do you know that Native youths like the two of you compose 70 percent of the youths admitted to the Federal Bureau of Prisons, despite the fact that Native youths make up only 1 percent of the country's youth population? In our home state of Alaska, where Native Peoples compose 16 percent of the state population—the highest percentage of Native residents in the country—a whopping 37 percent of prisoners are Native! The incarceration rate is even higher for Alaska Native youth, who comprise 42 percent of all young offenders under State of Alaska custody!

So Malakas, when you asked me about *The New Jim Crow* last week I panicked a little bit, just like how I panicked when you asked me about *The Adventures of Huck Finn*. Last week though, your mom wasn't around to help me handle the situation, so I just squashed the conversation as quickly as I could. But now that I think about it, I think I squashed the conversation because you asking me about *The New Jim Crow* reminded me of a very dark, depressing, and unjust conceivable reality for you and Kaluguran. You asking me about the book made me very afraid. That moment made me very nervous about the two of you—my two Native sons—existing in this world.

And that is if you even make it to jail. I understand that it's a sad, disturbing, and infuriating situation for a parent to feel "lucky" and relieved because of the twisted reasoning, "although my child is in jail, at least he is alive." But that's exactly the kind of perverse and sickening reality we live in as Peoples of Color. And as Native boys, this especially applies to you and Kaluguran.

This is the cruel reality for those of us who are parents of Native children, that if—or based on research it might be "when"—we hear that our children got in trouble with the law somehow, we feel lucky and "thankful" that at least our child is alive and that he at least made it to jail.

You see, similar to how Black people are the victims in 26 percent of all police shootings, even though Black people make up only around 14 percent of the country's population, you need to become aware that Native Peoples are also victims of police killings in staggeringly disproportional rates. You need to know the stories of Christopher J. Capps, Paul Castaway, Nicholas "Sul" Concha, Mah-Hi-Vist Good-blanket, Rexdale W. Henry, Kenneth John, Corey Kanosh, Allen Locke, Joseph Murphy, Benjamin Whiteshield, John T. Williams, Detlef Wulf, and many others.

You need to know the story of Vincent "Pamiuq" Nageak III—your uncle Pum.

These Native males represent just a small and recent fraction of the many Native individuals who have been killed by law enforcement officers. You need to know that Native Peoples account for almost 2 percent of all victims of police killings, despite the fact that Native Peoples compose only .8 percent of the United States population. This means that Native Peoples—like you—are the most at-risk of being killed by law enforcement.

These are your realities, and they scare the hell out of me.

So Malakas—please pay attention. Please listen.

Please set a good example for your brother. As his Kuya—his older brother—please help me to get him to pay attention and to listen. Please help him.

Historical trauma has wounded your ancestors, and their wounds haven't yet healed. As Filipino and Native boys, your traumatic colonized histories and their ugly legacies have put you at risk for many unwanted outcomes already. I am worried about what might happen to you in this world, and consequently, I am worried about the potential damages you may inflict not only to yourself but also to others. My sons, you were already weighed down before you even got started in this world. And if these historical burdens haven't already messed you up, this modern world probably will do.

This world is not lenient; it won't give you many second chances. This world will frustrate you, test you, and provoke you. And if you get fed up, resist, and fight back, this world is quick to punish you, perhaps even kill you.

These are the reasons why I am so demanding, the reasons I am so strict. These are the reasons why I need to be tough and serious.

Because you are Native boys. Because you are Filipino boys.

Because I am in fear. Because I am terrified.

I'm sorry.

IV. MY DAUGHTER

Let us not seek to satisfy our thirst for freedom by drinking from the cup of bitterness and hatred.

—Martin Luther King Jr.,
I *Have a Dream Speech*
(August 28, 1963)

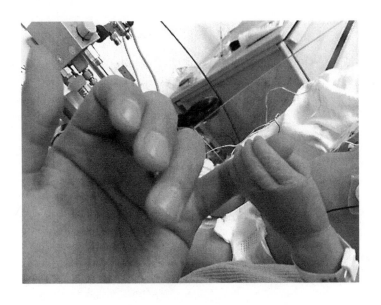

*In the Alaska Native Medical Center Neonatal
Intensive Care Unit when Kalayaan was born.*

April 20, 2016

My Daughter,

You were born two months early, a "preemie," according to the world. This term is short for "premature," meaning you did not get to the point of maturity. So the connotation of being a preemie is that you are not mature enough, and so therefore, you are behind. And given my relative ignorance concerning matters of infant development, I believed the warnings, and so I expected and prepared myself for your delayed development.

During your first months operating on this earth, trying to sense it and figure it out, I interpreted your behaviors using the preemie framework. I remember when you were just barely over one year old, and as we were getting ready to get out the door, you rushed to put your shoes and coat on, and brought your Kuya his shoes and coat to put on. I saw this behavior—and your general eagerness to help and do well—as you simply trying to keep up because you were already behind. I thought you were just overcompensating to mask your failure to meet "developmental milestones" and expectations.

But I was wrong.

It took me a couple of years, but I eventually realized that you are not behind at all. When I look back on your early birth now, I see that the reason you came to us earlier than we were expecting—and the reason why you were so willing and ready to get going—is because you were ahead.

You were not premature; you were ahead of schedule. You were ahead of the "normal" timeline that this earth, this society, this culture has come up with. You are not eager to learn new things so you can catch up; you've already got it and are just ready to move on to what's next. You aren't overcompensating to make up for anything; you are already ahead of everybody else, and so going above and beyond what was expected just comes easily, naturally, and effortlessly for you.

Right from the beginning, you showed me that you are free from how this world wants to categorize and put restrictions on you. The world says you're premature, but your behaviors said, "Nope, I'm advanced." The world said you got here too early and that you're not ready, but you said, "Nope, your timeline is just slow and behind." Kalayaan—now I know—you have always been super-mature, ahead, and well beyond your years. You are wise.

Your Grandpa David even called you "Dolly" when you were a baby—his own play at the "Dalai Lama"—because your quiet, knowing eyes just exuded wisdom.

You just seem like you know more than you can express. You just seem like you know.

For instance, one of the defining moments for me that attests to how advanced you are—and how much you are already able to teach me—happened when you were around three years old. You see, over the first couple of years of your life, I came to habitually say to you things like "You're such a pretty girl" or "Hi pretty girl!" Then, during one night while going through our bedtime routine, we had a brief conversation that went something like this.

E.J.: You ready to go night-night, pretty girl?

KALAYAAN: (You put your hands gently on my face and calmly said) Dad, I don't want to be pretty girl anymore.

E.J.: Oh, well, what do you want to be?

KALAYAAN: I just, I just, I just want to be Cool Kalayaan.

E.J.: Well, being pretty can be cool.

KALAYAAN: Well, I just want to be cool. Just Cool Kalayaan.

It seems simple and quite ordinary, but that moment has stuck with me because it made me seriously reflect on the messages that I—in both subtle and blatant ways—was conveying to you as a human being who happens to be female. That night, I went to bed thinking about what standards, expectations, roles, and values I may be imposing on you but not on your brothers.

That night, I began to think about—and worry about—what this world will impose on you as a female, and as a Filipina and Native female. It terrified me.

But at the same time, that night gave me a glimpse of how you are already resisting the legacies of oppression that I was unintentionally—perhaps even well-intentionally—passing on to you. That night, in your own simple and quiet yet powerful way, I saw how you were already trying to escape historical and modern-day impositions.

That night, although still just a three year old, it seemed like you already knew and that you were already breaking free.

✦ ✦ ✦

Kalayaan, I am not sure if now is the right time to talk to you and your brothers about the dark, painful, and depressing realities of this world. As I write this, your Kuya Malakas is not even seven yet and you are barely five. Our bunso, Kaluguran, is the youngest at three years old, and I can't even have any kind of conversation with him beyond him telling me that he's a big boy when he's told to take a nap, and then him telling me that he's a baby again when he's told to feed himself. So talking to him about racism right now is definitely out of the question.

As you and your brothers are mixed-race children of color, I know that it is a necessity for me and your mom to talk to you about race and racism. To be silent about race and racism, or to pretend that they no longer matter, is not only a lie and may not only lead to normalizing injustice and leaving it unchallenged, but it is also a disservice to you because you will eventually find out that it is very real and that it has very real consequences. I also understand that navigating race and racism, along with its intersections with other forms of "isms" such as sexism and heterosexism, should be an ongoing endeavor for our entire family and not just a one-time thing.

What I am not sure about is the appropriate age for you and your brothers to be exposed to, engaged in, and comprehend the complex, sensitive, and painful matter of these letters. I am not sure when the three of you will read these, or when you will be allowed to, but I hope it happens early. This is because I don't want you and your brothers to learn about the contents of these letters too late.

You see, Tamir Rice was only twelve years old when he was shot dead by Cleveland police. Aiyana Stanley-Jones was only seven years old when she was killed by Detroit police. This past summer, a fourteen-year-old girl was violently wrestled to the ground and kneeled on by Texas police. Just last week, twelve-year-old Janissa Valdez was body-slammed face first into the ground by a police officer while she was in school. A couple of years ago, an eight-year-old Native girl was tasered by four South Dakota Police Officers in her own home. Also in South Dakota earlier this year, fifty-seven Native kids between the ages of nine and thirteen years old were subjected to blatant racial slurs and were sprayed by beer while they were watching a hockey game. Over in Canada, an eight-year-old Filipino child was told by his teacher that his traditional Filipino eating habits were disgusting, and that he needed to learn to eat like Canadians. Statistics also show that Filipino and Native children are dehumanized and become victims of sexual abuse and exploitation at even younger ages. So I need you and your brothers to know about race and racism, soon.

But you all probably already know right now, at least to some limited extent. You see, research tells me that children already begin to notice basic differences between people—like skin color and hair color—by the time they are two years old. So I am sure that, by now, you and your brothers are already well-aware of these basic differences, as the family portraits you all like to draw always show me as having darker brown skin compared to the rest of you all. I love these portraits, by the way.

Also, I am pretty sure that your awareness of differences between people extends to differences between groups of people, as research also shows that when children are around three to four years old they already begin to make generalizations about groups of people and to begin attaching societal messages—both positive and negative—about the characteristics we have learned to assume that they have. In other words, stereotypes and prejudices—or general patterns of organizing the world into categories and the relationships between such categories—tend to develop quite early in our lives. Research also suggests that by the time we are three to four years old, we have been exposed to the world enough to already begin to internalize or believe what the world teaches us about others and ourselves, about other groups of people and about our own groups.

And these research findings are for typical children, which you are not. My Kalayaan, I am pretty sure you are already beyond these basic forms of racial awareness, so I am pretty sure you already know some of this. Sorry, I am *quite* sure.

Also, remember one of your favorite movies—*Inside Out*? I especially like this movie because it does an excellent job of dramatizing super-technical, daunting, and potentially boring scientific processes and presenting them to a general audience in an understandable, age-appropriate, palatable, and entertaining manner. As a lover of animated films who also happens to have training in clinical psychology, the many messages that the movie tries to impart—such as how our personalities or identities are complex and may be composed of various crucial parts, how our emotions can "color" our perception and interpretation of the world, and how shutting out and not experiencing sadness is not really the best way to be psychologically healthy—makes this easily one of my top-ten favorite animated films of all time.

As a brown-skinned Filipino American man who grew up in colonized Philippines and racialized United States of America, however, I think my inner workings are very different from Riley's—the eleven-year-old White protagonist in the movie. This "train of thought" led me to wonder about how your internal world and your brothers' internal world may be different from Riley's as well. Then, I thought about all of the different types of peoples who identify with a particular social group—and whose social group is an important part of their identity and personality—but whose social group is often inferiorized, discriminated against, othered, or marginalized by society; their psychological experiences are most likely very different from Riley's as well.

You see, for Riley's case, I wondered why she didn't have a "White People Island" as one of the significant parts of her identity, along with "Soccer Island," "Family Island," and "Goofball Island." Is it because research shows that White youths and youths of color are on very different developmental timelines in terms of racial identity development? Is it because research suggests that White people very rarely think about racial identity, if at all, or at least not as much as Peoples of Color? Kalayaan, not having the need to think about one's racial identity is a privilege that you and your brothers don't have, that our family does not have, as Peoples of Color.

I am not sure if the movie creators were even aware of this, let alone if they made deliberate decisions surrounding Riley's lack of racial identity development. But what I do know is that unlike White children like Riley, children of color like you typically become aware of race and racial identity by the time they are three to four years old. So I am quite sure that you and your brothers already have a "Filipino island" and "Native island" in your minds. I'm quite sure that you and your brothers have already begun to attach certain stereotypes, beliefs, and attitudes toward different groups of people, including the groups you belong to. I'm quite sure you and your brothers already know about race and have begun to already understand racism.

And again, these research findings are for typical children, which you are not. So my Kalayaan, my Filibascan daughter, you probably already know.

Kalayaan, because I'm quite confident that you already have a "Filipino island" and a "Native island" and a "Girl island," because these social groups are already important parts of your developing identity, and because how you regard these parts of your self is going to be influenced by the beliefs, attitudes, and stereotypes this world has about your social groups, I feel a strong sense of responsibility—as your parent—to share with you some of what I know about this world and what it will attach to you as a Filipina and as a Native female.

And although I know you already know and understand a lot more than other kids your age—and even though you have already taught me plenty about myself—please still allow me to share and teach you a few more things.

Kalayaan, you are a product of—and will forever be shaped by—your ancestors' colonized history. As I've shared with your brothers, historical trauma has wounded your ancestors, and their wounds haven't yet healed. These wounds continue to have very real effects on you today. You have the vestiges of intergenerational violence, hurt, and trauma in you—passed on to you by me and your mom. Just like your brothers, your identity and life are influenced by the colonized histories of your Filipino and Athabascan selves, putting you at added risk to develop feelings of shame and self-doubt about yourself and your heritage, which in turn may manifest in various ways such as alcohol and drug use, poor school performance, depression, and suicide. The soul wound or loss of kapwa can also manifest itself through interpersonal violence, especially among our peoples, as many of us express our frustrations, hurts, pains, and grief laterally on others who are like us—our own peoples—perhaps because our peoples remind us of our supposed inferiority, helplessness, and irrelevance.

The self-esteem issues and depression brought on by the soul wound or loss of kapwa may lead to other concerns such as body image problems, as research tells me that you might already begin to be dissatisfied with your body and be overly concerned about overeating as early as when you're in third grade. The self-esteem damage brought on by your colonized history may also lead to various high-risk behaviors. For instance, research tells me to worry about unintended pregnancy and sexually transmitted diseases, more so than your other Asian peers who are Chinese, Korean, Japanese, Indian, or Vietnamese. Research tells me too that you are very likely to think about suicide, or perhaps run away, or be taken away, and become a victim of human sex trafficking. Yes, my Filibascan daughter, child sex-trafficking that caters to White men is a huge, profitable "industry" in the Philippines; here in the United States, you are also at highest risk for sex-trafficking as a Native female.

And there seems to be an interactive effect of you being both Filipino and Native too! As mixed-race kids in Alaska, research tells me that you and your brothers are most likely to use alcohol and are at very high risk for binge drinking. As mixed-race kids, you and your brothers are also most likely to smoke marijuana and use cocaine, solvents, heroin, methamphetamines, or ecstasy. Data also tells me that you are the most likely to be bullied in school, and the most likely to feel sad and hopeless. As mixed-race kids, research suggests that you and your brothers are most likely to seriously consider killing yourselves and plan a suicide attempt.

As a female, research tells me that you are very likely to experience violence, especially the domestic kind. Data shows that half of all women in our home state of Alaska experience either intimate partner violence or sexual violence or both, with Native women being at even higher risk for being victimized. In other words, when I look at you and your mom, research tells me that one of you will face violence. I know your mom has never experienced any form of that, and I sure hope she never will. So then I worry about you.

And if you do become a victim of violence, it doesn't look like this world will be much help to you. It doesn't look like the systems we have right now will facilitate healing and justice in any way.

You see, this world has a reputation for not valuing the lives of women, especially the lives of women of color, especially the lives of Native women—like you. For instance, there are numerous occurrences of violence and crimes against Native women being ignored, swept under the rug, or not being prioritized by law enforcement officials. In our home state of Alaska, for example, where we have the highest rate of rape compared to all other states in the country, and where Native females like you have a one-in-three chance of being raped, only 29 percent of reported rapes result in an arrest—of which only 69 percent continue on to prosecution. Another egregious example of this devaluation of Native women's lives is the Canadian government's refusal to pay attention to and prioritize the alarming statistics regarding First Nations women: that although they compose only 4 percent of Canada's female population, First Nations women are 25 percent of all homicide victims, 16 percent of female murder victims, and 11 percent of missing women! In total, the Royal Canadian Mounted Police reported that there are at least 1,181 indigenous women who were either murdered or are missing over the past thirty years. This suggests that one Native woman has gone missing or is murdered every ten days over the past thirty years, and no one is taking it seriously enough! The United Nations Committee on the Elimination of Discrimination against Women stated that such "victimization of Native women is partly the legacy of colonial heritage..." and that the lack of attention to it is "a grave violation" of indigenous women's rights.

In addition to the negative legacies of your colonized past, you are also a product of our contemporary society's perceptions and stereotypes about Filipinos, about Natives, about Filipinas and Native women. You will become aware of mail-order bride and Pocahontas jokes. You will face the "submissive Filipina" and "sexy Indian" stereotypes. People will commend you on your English fluency, saying things like, "Your English is so good, you don't sound Filipino," or something like, "You're so articulate, you don't talk like a Native person." Or someone might say to you that, "You're pretty for a Native girl." Or someone might ask you even after you already said that you were born in the United States: "No, where are you really from?" Or someone, even a well-meaning and lifelong friend, might introduce you to new people as "My Filipino friend" or "My Native friend," or perhaps, "My Eskimo." Or someone might make you their mascot, and then tell you not to be too sensitive because it is well-intentioned, that it is to honor you and your people.

And the devaluation of your heritage goes beyond the interpersonal level to also be reflected in our systems. For example, in our home state of Alaska, right now we have Supreme Court justices who believe that Alaska Native life is not real, that village life is not valid. We have Supreme Court justices who trivialize and degrade Alaska Natives Peoples' cultural, spiritual, and religious connections to their villages and their subsistence life. We have Supreme Court justices who regard the Native ways of living as not "reality," asserting that people who choose to live traditionally according to their Native ways are just on a vacation similar to privileged folks who go on a "retreat in Tibet." These are examples of interpersonal and systemic forms of microaggression, and research shows that individuals who are members of marginalized groups frequently experience plenty of microaggression in their everyday lives. Even further, research also shows that these modern-day experiences of subtle oppression can lead to feelings of shame, doubt, inferiority, depression, and various other concerns.

As you can see, racism and sexism are alive and well in today's world—which adds on to the risk factors and damages inflicted on you by the colonized histories of your ancestors—and research tells me that all of such ugliness has serious negative effects on your health and other indicators of well-being, such as educational attainment, income, and life satisfaction. As a Woman of Color, you will experience heightened levels of stress that not only will put you at higher risk for poorer health, but such interactive and cumulative racism- and sexism-related stress will also negatively affect your children's health as well! For instance, research shows that the racism and sexism that Women of Color experience on a regular basis are related to higher likelihood of preterm labor and low birth weight, both of which are related to various negative health outcomes. Is this what happened with your mom that led to your preterm birth? Research suggests that is definitely plausible. So you see, the consequences of past and present-day oppression are very real and deadly, not just for you as a Woman of Color but for your potential children too. You need to understand this, Kalayaan, and you need to resist all such oppression and struggle to remain free of all its harmful effects.

But please be careful when you do speak up and stand up against racism, sexism, and other forms of unfair treatment. Be very careful when you resist oppression and assert your freedom, because research also tells me that a Woman of Color like you are most likely to be punished for doing so. And data suggests that women of color are punished very harshly and disproportionately! For instance, similar to their male counterparts, Black women also face injustice with regard to the justice system. Specifically, although composing only around 13 percent of the United States female population, Black women make up 30 percent of the female prisoners in the country.

Similar to Black women, Native females like you are also disproportionately represented in the prison system. For example, in South Dakota and Montana where Native Peoples compose 8 percent and 6 percent of the state population, respectively, Native women comprise 35 percent and 25 percent of such states' female prison population. In our home state of Alaska, where Native Peoples compose 16 percent of the state population, 35 percent of female prisoners are Native. According to the Lakota Peoples Law Project, Native women are six times more likely to be admitted to prison than White women. Furthermore, Native female adolescents have the highest incarceration rate among all racial groups, and they are five times more likely than White girls to be admitted into a juvenile detention facility!

And parallel to my fears about your brothers, this fear that I have about you ending up in jail is perversely qualified with the painful truth that you may even be considered "lucky" to make it to jail alive once you interact with police. My Filibascan daughter, you need to know that other Native women such as Sarah Lee Circle Bear, Jacqueline Salyers, Christina Tahhahwah, Loreal Tsingine, and many others were not "lucky" enough to make it to jail alive. So be careful when you do resist, speak up, and educate. Be careful when you assert your freedom.

Kalayaan, please don't get me wrong. Of course I encourage you and your brothers to keep trying, to achieve, and to be all that you can be. I encourage you to be strong, to keep fighting, and to remain free. After all, you are privileged in many ways. As Americans, as children of highly educated parents, as lighter-skinned people, and as children who are growing up in a relatively stable and loving home, you have opportunities that many kids in America, in the Philippines, and all over the world do not even know exist.

But you should always remember—you and your brothers should plant it permanently in your minds and hearts—that no matter how "successful" you may get or "respectable" you may think you have become, you are still Peoples of Color. You, Kalayaan, are still a Woman of Color.

You need to know that we still live in a country wherein a woman earns seventy-nine cents to every dollar a White man earns. To make it even worse, Women of Color are paid even lower; Black Women in Alaska get only sixty-four cents, Latinas in Alaska get only fifty-eight cents, American Indian and Alaska Native Women get only fifty-nine cents, and Asian Women in Alaska get only fifty-four cents for every dollar paid to a White man. And this wage gap— which really is just another manifestation of how much women, especially Women of Color, are devalued in our country—holds true regardless of industry, occupation, and level of education.

So you and your brothers should work hard. You all should impress people, get them to like you, to accept you, and to respect you. I am sure you can accomplish all of these things, because I see that you work so hard and determinedly to accomplish them now. But always be on guard and be in touch with the reality that this world's standards of acceptability, respectability, and desirability are constantly moving targets for Peoples of Color—especially for Women of Color like you, Kalayaan.

You need to always remember that being a respected college professor did not save Ersula Ore from being seriously roughed up by police. You need to remember that a high level of education did not save Dr. Martin Luther King Jr. Being a Christian—a pastor at that—didn't seem to matter for him either. Wearing suits and ties and being articulate did not save Malcolm X. Serving the country through the military certainly did not save Medgar Evers. Graduating from Harvard and Yale, being a professor of constitutional law, and having a White American woman for a mother did not spare Barack Obama from being questioned about his qualifications, birth place, and citizenship. There are many more examples—historically and contemporarily—of "respectable" Black people who were nevertheless stereotyped, mistreated, doubted, suspected, and even killed simply because they were Black. Such examples tell us that level of education, popularity, how well one plays a certain sport, how much money one makes, how one dresses, how one speaks, how patriotic one is, what kind of music one listens to, or even how loud one plays his music, do not save Black lives.

Similarly, "respectability" does not save Native lives either. Here's an example: Vincent "Pamiuq" Nageak III, a proud Inupiaq man, was a U.S. Army veteran. He was the nephew of an Alaska State Representative, and his family is well-known and well-regarded in their hometown of Barrow. Pamiuq served as an officer for the Department of Corrections, working closely with the North Slope Borough Police Department for over 10 years, then transitioned into working for the North Slope Borough Fire Department, being named "Firefighter of the Year," and eventually becoming Fire Chief. He also ran for a City Assembly Seat and won. He also obtained a college degree while serving his community. He did all of these things while also hunting and whaling, staying true to his Inupiaq heritage and further making him a well-respected community member. Pamiuq did not criticize the justice system; he was part of the system. He did not campaign for the improvement of police work especially with regard to police brutality and racial inequalities. In fact, he liked T-shirts that said "I can breathe, because I don't break the law."

But none of these "respectable" things saved your Uncle Pum. He was shot dead by police, while he was inside his own home—alone.

So of course, reach for the sky. Go into whatever field or industry you are passionate about. Obtain the highest level of education that you want. I know you are free and capable to do all of such things. But always remember that, as a Woman of Color, respectability and being somewhat accepted or "mainstream" will still only get you so far in this world. Your freedom in this world is still limited and is still very much an illusion.

Many people, including very wise folks like James Baldwin and your mom, say that the limitations that this world imposes on you—or your brothers—do not mean that you are naturally inferior or mediocre or less. Instead, it speaks to the world's unjust, irrational, and misinformed beliefs about you and what you are capable of. And I agree with them wholeheartedly.

But my conviction on such a declaration is not enough; the volume and intensity with which I shout such a statement will not help you. What will help you is to know and understand the traumatic histories of our ancestors, the bleak reality of our present, and the many negative consequences such historical and contemporary oppression drops on us. Yes, it is painful, but it's the truth and it's necessary. You need to know and understand the truth or you will otherwise be forever caged in ignorance. You cannot break away and be free if you do not understand, or if you are not even aware, that you are trapped.

And Kalayaan, you have already made it clear to me— very poignantly—that you want to be free. Well, freedom is not easy. Freedom is not pain-free.

✦ ✦ ✦

It pains me to have to share these gloomy realities to you. It is infuriating as a parent to learn that you are at higher risk for a wide range of scary, violent, adverse, and undesirable outcomes simply because you are Filipina, Native, and female. And it makes me even madder to realize that many of these risk factors were passed on to you from the trauma that our ancestors experienced, through me. Even further, it is depressing to grasp the reality that—through my own ignorant actions, beliefs, and attitudes as a man—I have undoubtedly, even if unintentionally or perhaps even well-intentionally, contributed to your oppression in one form or another. I am sorry.

Kalayaan, you love swimming, so I'll give you a swimming metaphor. Imagine yourself in a river, trying to make it to fish camp. Because you are Filipina and Native, you are swimming upriver against the current, while carrying the sandbags of colonialism. In addition, you also have twigs and rocks and tree branches blocking your way and drifting toward you, scratching you, poking your eye, or trying to drown you. These obstructions represent the barriers that this contemporary world has set up for you because you are Filipina and Native. This is why you and your brothers cannot have second chances, why you cannot make mistakes. As Native and Filipino kids you don't have that luxury. This world will not give you many chances; any mistake you make in this world can cost you—perhaps even kill you.

And you, Kalayaan, because not only are you Filipino and Native but you are also female, you have even more twigs and rocks and tree branches trying to drown you. And because I am a colonized man who has internalized racist, paternalistic, and heteronormal standards, I am one of those twigs, rocks, and tree branches—especially if

I choose not to be aware of this reality, if I deny this reality, if I minimize this reality.

The reality is that these twigs, rocks, and tree branches are everywhere, and many people—men and women—do choose to be willfully ignorant about such reality and their complicit and implicit roles in them. This is why I am very scared for you. I am terrified now and I am petrified about your future.

You see, as I write this, the clear favorite to become the Republican Party's presidential candidate is a man named Donald Trump who has campaigned on explicitly bigoted and chauvinistic principles, yet remains overly popular among millions of our fellow Americans. Let me be clear—I'm not scared of Donald Trump; one person holding bigoted views isn't new or threatening. In a country as diverse and as populated as the United States, we're bound to have outliers. Besides, bigotry—whether it be racism, sexism, heterosexism, xenophobia, Islamophobia, ableism, or others—has always been around and has always been very real. So one person holding bigoted views isn't scary. What scares me is to realize that Donald Trump is not a statistical outlier at all. What scares me is that bigotry seems to be the norm instead of an exception. What terrifies me is to realize that I'm surrounded by millions of people who not only may hold such bigoted views and find them acceptable, but who are also invigorated by them. Donald Trump is just an ugly symptom of a long-held, widespread, and very deadly disease.

The disease that millions of people in our midst seem to be infected with—a disease that they can use to seriously hurt you, me, our family, and our loved ones—is what scares me. It terrifies me that we seem to be surrounded by this disease. This is why I am scared for you, my Filibascan daughter, living in this disease-infested world.

But believe it or not, as terrified as I am about you living, surviving, and thriving in this racist, patriarchal, misogynistic world, I have been even more frightened than this. Kalayaan, the scariest time of my life was approximately five years ago, when you were born two months ahead of schedule. Sure, I've experienced many other distressing situations—and a big chunk of my life has been lived in constant anxiety and paranoia—but the eight-week period surrounding your birth was when I was the most scared, because I was scared to lose you.

Those few weeks of uncertainties regarding your health—your life—were so frightening to me that, after we were able to get through it, I felt like I could get through anything. I felt strong. So a few months after that ordeal I ran my first marathon—with a torn ACL—because temporary, nonfatal, physical pain was nowhere close to the deep, lifelong, emotional agony I was fearing, and luckily escaped. Losing you—even just the thought of it—is much more painful than anything this world can ever do to me. It was almost as if I was desensitized, and at that time I felt brave to face whatever ugliness this world has to throw toward me. I felt like I had nothing to lose!

But whatever strength and bravery I had faded away quickly, it didn't last long, because the reality is that I didn't lose you, Kalayaan. You fought hard and now that I have you living in this world, I realize that I actually have way more to fear. Now that you are here, I have way more to lose! I can still lose you! And given the bleak statistical forecasts for you as a Filipina and Native female, this world is definitely frightening!

So I went back to being terrified. But just last week while I was running, and memories of pain, the marathon, fears, racism, depressing statistics for Native and Filipino Peoples, violence, deaths, and your Uncle Pum came back flooding into my consciousness, I asked myself why I was so scared to lose you five years ago? Why was I so scared of you dying and leaving this world? If I see this world as so unjust and unfair, bleak and hopeless, then why was I so scared that you were not going to experience it?

This is when I realized that, despite everything, I still want you to have a chance. I still want you to live in this world and experience its many beauties. I still want you to get your shot at making this world a better place. Because I believe in you. Because despite the "risk factors" and the un-desirables, I also see the protective factors and the awesome things about our Peoples. I also see the resiliency factors; I see what makes us strong and fierce. I wanted you to live in this world because I still see that our Peoples have plenty to contribute to heal this world, and the contributions and healing can come through you. I wanted so badly for you to be here in this world despite its ugliness, because deep down, I still believe that this world has a chance.

I realize now that you—and your brothers and other contemporaries—are that chance.

I realize now that you wanted so badly to be in this world that you couldn't wait to get here; you wanted so badly to be in this world and get a shot at it that you came early. You wanted so badly to be in this world that you must have a purpose, and to me that purpose seems to be to bring hope, freedom, and healing.

This world imposed labels and assumptions on you right when you were born, but you broke free from such limitations. Right from the get-go, by demonstrating that it's possible to be free of the artificial restrictions this world has enforced on us for many generations, you have taught me that there's hope for you in this world, and therefore, there's still hope for me and there's still hope for our Peoples.

Kalayaan, through my short five years of knowing you so far, I have already learned and changed so much. I have begun to see my privilege as a man, and I hope you will continue to help me as I struggle—perhaps eternally—to keep my male privilege in check. But I do understand that it is not your responsibility to constantly educate me about my privilege, just like I find it taxing and unfair that people seem to constantly put on me the burden of educating White people of my and my ancestors' humanity. So it's fine if you so choose to let me struggle on my own. You have already done enough in your young life by sparking a sense of awareness within me, making me realize that with ignorance and blindness—even unintentional or well-intentional—I can contribute to your oppression. Through this, you taught me that I—we—can be free of how we were socialized. You taught me that, although not easy, we can break free of the "maladaptive" attitudes, thoughts, and behaviors that we have developed because of colonialism and contemporary oppression. You taught me that I can change my perspective as a privileged man, and so you taught me that change can and does happen in this world.

Yes, I am still very scared and terrified. I am still very much aware of the ugliness and bleakness of our world. I am still very conscious of the frighteningly harsh reality facing you as a Woman of Color. I still feel the widespread serious threat on the well-being of our Peoples. I still am painfully aware of my own imperfections, damages, fears, limitations, weaknesses, and insecurities. I still see the desolation facing us, our families, and our communities. But now I also see a small glimmer of hope. I see that we still have a shot.

Kalayaan, you have taught me that despite my colonized history and lived experiences, despite my deeply ingrained internalized inferiority and developed anxieties, and despite the many instances during which I have inflicted damage not only to myself but also onto other people, I can still break free from the legacies and effects of oppression.

Thank you.

V. OUR ROOTS

We have not stopped trembling yet, but if we had not loved each other none of us would have survived. And now you must survive because we love you, and for the sake of your children and your children's children.

—James Baldwin,
The Fire Next Time
(1963)

*Malakas's drawing of the family with Kaluguran—
and love—in the center.*

May 30, 2016

Our Roots,

My dear family, our roots have been damaged.

Generations of colonial violence have injured our ancestors, and their injuries haven't yet healed. Such historical violence and the wounds they have inflicted on our ancestors' bodies, minds, and souls are not commonly known, acknowledged, or given much importance; sometimes they are even denied, distorted, minimized, or forgotten altogether—further worsening the wounds and their many negative effects.

My love, these wounds and the consequent infections and comorbidities have been passed on to me and you. The continued inferiorization of our roots that we more proximally and directly experienced further exacerbated our inherited wounds, seeping even deeper into our minds and our souls, fooling us into automatically thinking and believing that there is something inherently wrong with who we are, our cultures, our Peoples. Because it has been so strongly hammered into us for so long, it has become an unnoticed part of us—like a parasite—continuing to damage us and kill us outside our awareness. And because of this insidiousness, we have undoubtedly—even if unintentionally or well-intentionally—passed on these infected, parasitic, and dangerous wounds along with their many poisons to our children.

My love, it took us a long time to get to this level of awareness—to acknowledge the existence of colonial mentality, the soul wound, and the loss of kapwa—and to understand that our roots and our Peoples are not naturally inferior. You and I both know that we went through plenty of tears, heartaches, tensions, and physical, emotional, and spiritual pains—together and independently of each other—just to get to this point of acknowledging the bleakness of our historical and contemporary realities. And we both know that our struggles have persisted and will continue, perhaps for the rest of our lives.

We have become aware of the fact that there's nothing natural about racism, xenophobia, sexism, or other forms of social group oppression. We learned that there is enormous, deliberate, and intentional social, psychological, cultural, and infrastructural work that went into creating an oppressive society. Similarly, you and I have fought hard to get to the awareness that being ashamed and embarrassed of our roots, feeling inferior, unattractive, and undesirable because of our roots, and desiring to rid ourselves of our roots are not natural. We had to put in tremendous cultural, psychological, and spiritual work to recognize that we were not born hating ourselves and our heritage and our Peoples. We have struggled to understand that we cannot accept oppression, we can't just let it go, and we definitely can't internalize it. We have learned that we need to resist it. Every day.

This consciousness of the battles we constantly face has defeated me and depressed me, my love. Oppression's redundancy has taken a toll on me and has permanently damaged me. It has made me feel hopeless. I am quite sure you've had similar periods of desolation, although you seem to handle it better than me. I say this because despite experiencing similar struggles, you seem to have a little bit more than I do and you are still able to share some of what you have—like your wisdom and optimism—with me.

You see, you've helped me recognize that we are not alone in our struggles. I realized that many other Filipinos share the same difficulties as me; you helped me realize that Filipinos are not alone in their collective experience of colonialism and cultural genocide. With you, I continued to learn that racial and ethnic minority groups are not alone in their experiences of social group oppression. You helped me develop a sense of connectedness with other people, even people who on the surface may seem to not have any similarities with me. You've helped me regain, strengthen, and value my kapwa.

But although such connectedness make me feel less alone, it doesn't necessarily help that much in making me feel less weak, less vulnerable, and less depressed. In fact, realizing the pervasiveness of oppression and the depth of its damages has made me feel even more helpless, more at risk, and more disheartened.

And my love, as I've become aware—as I've become conscious of the historical and contemporary pains of our roots—you have been always quick to remind me of the positives as well. You have been keeping me balanced.

You remind me that we are our ancestors. You tell me that, yes, our ancestors have wounds that have yet to heal. But you also tell me that our ancestors—our roots—have plenty of positives and strengths as well. And because we are our ancestors, we also carry with us today their positives, their resiliencies, their strengths.

You constantly remind me that we are descendants of people who, despite their imperfections, still persisted, survived, and *even loved* despite unimaginable cruelties and injustices. You regularly remind me that our ancestors and their resilience are in us, propelling our hearts and souls every second. You constantly remind me that we have the necessary strength and resolve to fight and get through whatever nastiness we face today.

You taught me, and relentlessly remind me, of the resilience and strengths of our Peoples. And through this, I learned that as damaged as our roots are, and as negative and unhealthy as such damages have been to our ancestors and the succeeding generations, our roots are still our most important protective factor. I learned over time the paradox that although it is our damaged roots that *have become* our most significant risk factor, our roots *are still* also our strongest shield to defend us from the potential harms of historical and contemporary oppression. Yes, our roots are damaged, but we need to appreciate how they have still survived. Our roots, despite centuries and generations of degradation and oppression, are still what holds us up today.

Research even supports this, my love. For example, there are consistent research findings to suggest that critical awareness and understanding of one's heritage, being connected to one's heritage, being involved and participating in one's heritage, having positive views and attitudes toward one's heritage, and being able to competently function and operate in one's heritage are related to better physical, emotional, mental, and spiritual well-being among Peoples of Color. Even further, research also shows that enculturation and strong ethnic or cultural identity are related to better educational and social outcomes.

But despite the fact that I understand the research, despite the fact that I am aware of the positive aspects of our roots that can serve as protective factors against the painful burdens imposed by oppression, and despite the fact that I know there are many other people in this world who experienced brutality, exploitation, and injustices and yet have displayed amazing resiliency to still survive and thrive, it's not easy to be conscious of the positives and strengths. I have to persistently, effortfully, and deliberately remind myself of the positives and strengths. And as I said earlier, this requires so much effort and determination that many times I can't even do this by myself; many times I need your help to get me through the darkness and still see the positives and strengths!

I am sorry, my love, for always having to depend on you to keep me balanced. It is maddening—and depressing—that what is supposed to be natural, effortless, and automatic to me is instead very laborious. And this strenuous work of remembering the positives and strengths of our Peoples became even more arduous and seemingly impossible after Pum's tragic death, as all the historical and contemporary oppression of our Peoples became even more salient and further darkened my perspective of this world. It just seems so hopeless. It all just seems like an illusion. Right now, it just feels like we are merely fooling ourselves into believing that there is hope, that change is possible, that things will get better. All the evidence shows that the systems and institutions and climates that oppress us and keep us down are very well-developed, but there is really no clear, effective, and solid blueprint for how to get out of this mess!

Perhaps this deep desolation will pass. I am certain, however, that this is not going to be the last time that I will sink and struggle. Perhaps the current wretchedness of my mind, heart, and soul is temporary, but I am sure this world will bring me back to a similar level of misery again. I can count on this world to do that. There will be other times when our worldviews will be disregarded. There will be other times when our languages and accents will be mocked. There will be other times when our lives will seem to not matter. There will be other times when the color of our skin will lead us to be treated unfairly. There will be other times when our heritage will put us at risk. My love, this is not going to be the last time that I will struggle to value our roots. There will be many other times when this world will overwhelm consciousness and connectedness, and make it very difficult for me to see the positives and strengths of our roots. That's just how oppression is; it's redundant.

Don't get me wrong; I value consciousness and connectedness. In fact, I believe they are the foundations of any personal and collective journey toward healing. I fought to gain consciousness—kamalayan, in my Tagalog language—of the historical and contemporary realities of my Peoples. Now as a scholar and researcher, I am fortunate and privileged to have resources and capabilities to continually expand, refine, and develop critical kamalayan. You have helped me extend this consciousness toward seeing the importance of connectedness—a stronger kapwa—to feel the reality that I am not alone and that many Peoples from across the world share similar struggles.

So yes, consciousness can be a good thing. And yes, connectedness can be a good thing. But being conscious of the widespread pains that have been going on for generations can also lead to a sense of loss, grief, helplessness, and hopelessness. Consciousness and connectedness do not necessarily lead to strength. In fact, they can lead to a sense of defeat and worthlessness. Consciousness and connectedness do not necessarily set me free from the chains of trauma, of cultural genocide, of colonial mentality. In fact, they can lead to a sense of inescapability, apathy, irresponsibility, and lack of agency. Consciousness and connectedness do not necessarily lead to peace. In fact, they can lead to anger, resentment, bitterness, vengefulness, and violence—both toward one's self and toward others.

So no, consciousness and connectedness are not enough for our personal and collective journeys to heal from historical and contemporary oppression. Consciousness and connectedness are not enough in this world, a world that still does not make it easy to see the positives and strengths of our roots. In this world, consciousness and connectedness are not enough for us to resist the continued oppression of our Peoples, to break free from the ugly legacies that oppression inflicted on our Peoples, and create enough change so that the next generations of Peoples are in a much better position than us. This world does not make it easy to have hope.

But, my love, I think we have more help now. You and I—together—have literally created a little bit more hope. I hope.

✦ ✦ ✦

Malakas, Kalayaan, Kaluguran—our roots, our ancestors, were damaged. So your mom and I are damaged. I know I am damaged, even permanently. Call me pessimistic. Call me realistic. Call me dramatic. Call me confused and conflicted. I am not sure what I am; I am still trying to figure that out, perhaps eternally. But what I do know is that I am a product of my environment, and this environment is cruel and unjust. And just like me, you are going to be products of this cruel and unjust world too.

A big part of your world is what your mom and I are able to provide for you. We know we are damaged, so the world we are able to provide you may not be ideal; in the very least, your mom and I know that the environment we are able to provide you will have more complications—some might say more obstacles—than the worlds of other children whose roots, ancestors, and Peoples were not as damaged and forgotten as ours.

In addition to our microsystems and mesosystems, our immediate circles, you will also have a world that is beyond the one you share with your mom and me. This outside world is composed of the belief systems, customs, worldviews, and institutions that permeate and impact everything about us and our immediate circles. As I've shared with you already, this contemporary world is so broken, so dangerous, and so unfair for folks like us that I am terrified of it. I've felt the pains this world can inflict on the soul, the mind, and the body. This larger world has not been, and still is not, very kind to our roots. In fact, this larger world has deeply damaged our roots.

Despite the relatively bad hand you were dealt, however, I hope that you appreciate how your mom and I are trying our very best to reduce the "risk factors" you inherited from us. Our goal, which is probably not any different from how other parents are raising their children, is to raise you in a way in which you won't have the need to recover from your childhood experiences. Probably unlike many other parents, however, your mom and I also constantly worry about how your childhood experiences are likely to be impacted by your ancestors' experiences. You see, while many other parents do deal with typical daily hassles of living, they probably don't have to also regularly deal with having to effortfully, mindfully, cautiously, and deliberately assess how their damaged roots may be manifesting in everything they think, say, do, and convey to their children. Many other parents probably don't need to worry as much as your mom and I do about how our damaged roots may manifest among the three of you. Probably unlike many other parents, your mom and I have to constantly hold a certain level of suspicion toward our own Peoples—as awkward and painful but understandable and necessary as this may be—because we are afraid that our damaged roots might have damaged them enough to hurt you. Malakas, Kalayaan, Kaluguran—not only do I wish that you didn't have to live in this world having to overcome barriers that many other kids don't have to overcome, I also wish you didn't have to go through this world having to recover from your ancestors' wounds.

So beginning with us, your mom and I are trying to break the vicious cycles of alcoholism, of violence, of abuse, of self-doubt, of worthlessness, of depression, of suicide. We are trying to no longer just be a vessel that intergenerationally infects you with the soul wound, with the loss of kapwa, with colonial mentality. We are trying our very best to not let oppression and its many negative effects seep into your mind, soul, and body.

We don't want you to internalize the oppression that our Peoples have been experiencing for generations, because internalized oppression can immensely hurt individuals and communities! For instance, one of the more publicized and tragic examples of this is when a biracial Asian-White American young man killed six people and injured fourteen others during a rampage in Isla Vista, California two years ago. In the killer's manifesto, there were plenty of instances wherein he described experiences of racism and how internalized racism contributed to his harmful thoughts, emotions, and behaviors. The manifesto shows that the killer perceived being White as superior and most desirable, saw himself as superior to non-Whites because he is part-White, and also saw his non-White part to be a permanent marker of inferiority. He hated his Asian self; he hated himself. And so he killed himself.

In addition to self-hate, internalized oppression also leads to discriminating against others of the same or similar identity, perhaps because other people serve as reminders of one's own perceived inescapable inferiority, or perhaps to distance one's self from who one may already perceive as inferior "others." This intragroup violence becomes intergroup violence when the hate is transferred to other groups who are also seen as inferior. So it's not surprising that three of the victims killed in Isla Vista were Chinese-Americans (intragroup), one was Mexican-American (intergroup), two were women (intergroup), and that the manifesto documented many instances of hatred toward women and Asian Americans, African Americans, and Latino Americans.

So you see, internalized oppression can lead us to hate ourselves and to hurt ourselves. It can also lead us to hate our communities and those who closely resemble us and therefore are closest to us—our family, friends, and other communities who share similar struggles with marginalization. Therefore, internalized oppression can lead us to hurt our communities, families, and friends. Internalized oppression has already damaged many Peoples throughout history, and tragedies such as Isla Vista remind us that internalized oppression continues to damage us.

Don't ever forget, however, that people are not born hating their heritage or hating themselves! Internalized oppression is learned, it is taught, and oppression is the teacher! Always remember that internalized oppression wouldn't exist without oppression. Internalized oppression is treacherous in that it fools us into thinking that the problem is in us, so that we blame ourselves for our own victimization, so that we hate ourselves and others who are like us, so that we end up destroying our own selves, our own Peoples, our own roots. In this way, internalized oppression is probably the most insidious manner in which oppression has damaged our roots.

So how do we protect ourselves from the ugly legacies and consequences of our damaged roots? My Filibascan children, I am not sure. Like I said, I am still confused. But what I have learned so far is that it helps tremendously to know, understand, and connect with our roots.

As damaged as our roots are, we cannot internalize and accept the inflicted damages and become ashamed of our roots. We cannot just give up our roots, forget them, abandon them, and replace them with what oppression tells us is better. Instead, we need to know our roots, understand them, and connect to them. Yes, my children, we break away by staying put. We break the cycles not by disappearing, running away, or forgetting our roots. We break the malicious cycles by planting our feet and hearts even more firmly on the ground, and by making this oppressive world see our survival, hear our realities, comprehend our fierceness, and feel our resilience. Your mom and I have learned—through our own personal experiences, through the stories of other people in our communities, and through empirical research—that our roots are our biggest, most important protective factor against historical and contemporary oppression! This is our dialectic, our tension, our paradox. This is our solution.

We rebel against the generations of beating inflicted on our heritage by digging our roots even deeper. We break away from the ugly legacies and effects of oppression by planting our feet even more strongly into the ground.

Your mom and I are trying to better know, understand, and be connected to our heritage so that we can pass on to you a stronger, more positive picture of your roots. So that you can use our roots to protect yourself from the violence that the larger society will throw at you. So that when they tell you you're ugly, you can tell them you're beautiful. So that when they tell you you're dumb, you can tell them you're smart. So that when they tell you you're dirty, you can tell them you're clean. So that when they laugh at you or ridicule you, you can tell them to stop. So that when they push you, you can push back. So that when they yell at you, you can yell right back. So that when they silence you, you can make even more noise. So that when they tell you you're backward, you can tell them you're ahead. So that when they don't let you in, you can tell them that you don't want to be in there to begin with. So that when they make you feel alone, you will remember that your Peoples are still here. So that when they ignore you or choose to not see you, you can shine even more. So that when they try to belittle you, you become even bigger. So that when they try to intimidate you and scare you, you know that our ancestors have prepared you for whatever. So that when they try to hurt you, you know that our Peoples have survived even worse suffering.

These are the reasons why it's important and essential for you to know, understand, and be connected to our roots despite this society's perpetual attempts to distort you, inferiorize you, dehumanize you, and erase you. So that you know better. So that you know the truth. So that you know who you are. So that you know who we are.

This may seem to you as very dark and pessimistic. You can make an argument that our contemporary world is more accepting and less dangerous than the one I experienced, and you are probably correct. Sure, despite my empirically based conviction that our damaged roots and this disease-infected social climate will undoubtedly affect you, I do understand that your world is different from mine and so how your world will influence your lives is a little different than how our roots and my experiences have influenced my life.

One of the bigger differences between your world and mine is technology; the technological climate the three of you were born into is dramatically different from the ones your mom and I grew up in. For example, your mom didn't grow up with cable television as she lived throughout rural Alaska. As for me, I grew up in the Philippines not having even a telephone in my home. To this day, I remember when I was around five or six years old, and I had to record myself on a cassette tape to share my daily stories and express my love to your Lolo who was already working in Alaska at that time. Then once the cassette tape—both sides—were filled up, your Lola would mail it up to Alaska. After your Lolo received and listened to my messages, several days or weeks later, he would record over the same cassette tape with his stories and expressions of love and mail it back to me and your Lola in the Philippines. Yeah, we used the same cassette tape repeatedly—recycled if you may—because that's the frugal way.

Anyway, this was how I "talked" to your Lolo in the 1980s. For me, it was very rare and a big deal when my neighbor—one of the few who had a telephone in their home—would scream for me to run to their house because

I got a long distance phone call from my father. But for you, you get bored with talking to the Philippines! For you, "Skyping" with the Philippines almost daily is normal. For the three of you, "Face Timing" is expected and you get confused when you cannot see the person you are talking to. Seeing the face of the person you are talking to even when they're thousands of miles away is your standard, your norm, your starting point.

And these drastic advancements in technology are some of the more important factors that will make your experiences and perspectives about race, about colonialism, about borders and immigration, about oppression, about our histories, and about our contemporary realities different from mine. The technology that you seem to be able to effortlessly learn and navigate through will be a huge help in your quest toward better understanding, appreciating, and valuing our roots. You are privileged enough to have access to and comprehend information about Koyukon Athabascan history and culture. You are privileged enough to have access to and comprehend information about Kapampangan, Tagalog, and Filipino histories and cultures. You are privileged enough to have the resources, to possess the capacity, and to be allowed to explore your roots.

When I was your age I didn't have anyone telling me about colonialism and its negative effects on my ancestors. I didn't have anyone telling me to be proud of my brown skin and my native tongue. I didn't have anyone helping me to positively regard and maintain my roots. I didn't have anyone emphasizing to me how important it is to be connected to our roots. But you, my Filibascan children, you are privileged enough to be surrounded by people who will encourage you, support you, and even expect you to be connected to your roots.

Beyond our immediate circles, you are also privileged enough in that when you look at the larger society you can see a slightly more welcoming and inspiring picture. That is, you can see that there are fewer glass ceilings trapping you, and the ones that are still there are a tad more fragile now. For instance, for your mom and me, our generation and those before us, having a Black man as president is an extreme outlier. But for the three of you, that's your norm! You don't know a country that has never had a Person of Color as president. And now as I write this, Hillary Clinton has become the first woman presidential nominee of a major political party, so we are as close as we have ever been to having a woman as president! And by this coming November, we may very well have the first woman president of the United States of America!

So your experiences with this world so far, my Filibascan children, is that we can have a mixed-race, Person of Color—man or woman—as president of our country! For your mom and me and those before us, this is drastically different from what we grew up with. But for the three of you it's the standard. For your mom and me, our generation and those who came before us, having a mixed-race, Person of Color man or woman as president was the goal—at least that's true for many of us. For you and your generation, it's not only your starting point, it is also all you know, what you expect, and—hopefully—what you want to improve on.

Even further, the three of you are privileged enough to be born in America. You have English as your first and primary language. You will not have an accent like me, you will not mix up your *p*'s and *f*'s and your *he* and *she* pronouns like me, and you will not have being "foreign born" as a barrier to you at all. You can travel almost anywhere in the world with your American passport and come back to America seamlessly. You can even claim to be truly indigenous to these lands! Shoot, you can even become the president of these lands!

Yeah, I remember being in election central in downtown Anchorage in 2008, when it became clear that Barack Obama was going to become the first Black president—the first mixed-race Person of Color president—of our country. The crowd was ecstatic, even emotional. An acquaintance of mine, a local James Brown impersonator, sobbed uncontrollably on my shoulder, as he was overwhelmed by a moment he never thought he would see in his lifetime. I also cried, thinking about how my future children—if I were ever blessed with any—would see an America wherein anything seemed possible for them. Just a few days later, your mom and I found out that we were pregnant with you Malakas. And so my optimism kept building; not only would my child be a natural-born American, he would also see an America wherein a mixed-race Person of Color—like him—could become president!

Malakas, Kalayaan, Kaluguran—right from when you were born you already had privileges, opportunities, and perspectives that are very different from mine. Just by simply being born in this country in these modern times, you already have privileges, opportunities, and perspectives that I never had and will never have. So my American children, your experiences are different and so your minds are shaped differently than mine. The connections in your brains are different than mine. Your norms and tendencies are different than mine. Hopefully, such differences will also lead to different hearts for you. So perhaps, there is hope for you. Perhaps there is hope for all of us.

But if you're going to leverage and risk your privileges and successfully embody this hope for our Peoples, the future generations, and Peoples who are not as privileged as you are—if you're going to help us progress instead of forgetting, minimizing, and therefore simply repeating the excruciating mistakes of the past—you need to be aware of what you are up against. And, my Filibascan children, what you are up against includes both the past and the legacies of the past that still persist in the present.

And to resist the damages of historical and contemporary oppression, you need to be connected to your roots. Further, in order to extend beyond personal transformation, protection, and healing—to go beyond yourself and also create positive change that will impact others and the following generations—you need strong, solid, liberated, and love-driven roots.

✦ ✦ ✦

My Filibascan children, you've probably noticed how I've been a little different lately. You've seen me bring out works written by Ta-Nehisi Coates, Michelle Alexander, Carlos Bulosan, James Baldwin, Harold Napoleon, Maya Angelou, Vine Deloria, W. E. B. DuBois, Eduardo Duran, Cornel West, Marilyn Frye, and others. You've probably noticed how I've been talking about brown skin, black skin, light skin, hate, love, and unfairness a lot more than usual. You've probably seen me cry—also a lot more than usual.

My loves, the past three months have been especially challenging. Everything that I've questioned, struggled with, and thought I've already resolved over my lifetime all came back. Your Uncle Pum's death and my struggles with it made me realize that I need something more than just kamalayan and kapwa. Perhaps I've always needed something more, but I just didn't know it until now. I thought I was already very critically aware and conscious, and because of this I thought I could withstand everything in this world. I thought being woke and being connected to and "in solidarity" with others were all I needed.

Kamalayan and kapwa may have been enough to wake myself up, to spark change within myself, to remain strong within myself because I know I am not alone, and to alter how and where I see myself in relation to others. They may have been enough to protect me for years. The time finally came, however, when kamalayan and kapwa were not enough to get me through, because kamalayan and kapwa combined with continued oppression just made me feel scared, trapped, and hopeless. I thought I was brave, free, and an effective agent of social change. But I wasn't. All I was doing was taking it and brushing it off. All I was doing was cowering and surviving.

And I can no longer be content with simply surviving. Being scared, trapped, and hopeless is not the transformation I want for myself; it is also not the transformation I want for you. I don't want you to be fearful and simply survive. I don't want to advise you to simply tolerate oppression, or to simply take it and brush if off. Don't get me wrong, consciousness and connectedness definitely transform individuals, and they can help you survive and not blame yourself for your own victimization. But consciousness and connectedness on their own do not transform much else beyond yourself. They are not enough to help and benefit anyone else beyond you. So I need something more. I need you to have more.

I also realized that kamalayan and kapwa combined with continued oppression just made me angry, hateful, vengeful, and potentially violent. Consciousness and connectedness that just simply leads to anger is not the transformation I want to have for myself. It is not the transformation I want you to have either. I am not encouraging you to know, understand, and be connected to our roots just to make you angry. And I definitely don't want you to be hateful and violent toward anyone. Don't get me wrong; consciousness and connectedness are necessary, but on their own are not enough. I need more. I need you to have more.

And so over the past three months I've struggled. I was searching for what can bring me some clarity, peace, and hope that I can pass on to you so that I can better prepare you for this unjust world. I was thinking about what I can share with the three of you so that you can be ready and hopefully withstand the ugly realities you are very much at risk for facing in this world. I was searching for advice that I can give you so that you not only survive but also thrive in this world. I was looking for something to give you so that you not only grow up to be positive members of society, but also agents of social change who will leverage and risk your privileges in working toward justice and equality.

So I reread books and journal articles, read new ones, watched films, and talked with mentors. I was trying to gather as much as I could with the hope that my senses and heart will capture something that will fill what I just most recently realized have been missing.

And, my loves, today I am still searching.

I still don't have any profound "wisdomy" answer to impart to you, and perhaps I never will. But what I do know today is that the three of you have something that I—that *we*—can use.

Malakas, the root of your name is "lakas," which means strength in our Tagalog language. Your hard-headedness that drives me nuts is a testament to your strength. It is evidence of your bravery that you tend to always stand up against imposing forces, including me. You are not afraid to question, to resist, to persist, to disrupt, to agitate, to talk back, to argue, to plead your case. With these observations, I realized that I need to be more like you. I cannot just keep protecting myself with my consciousness and connectedness. I cannot just keep putting up my shield as a cover against oppression. I can no longer just take it and brush it off, and just perpetually be on the defense. I cannot just merely strive to survive.

I recognize now that not only do I need strength for myself—so that I can simply withstand oppression and so that I can remember that I am connected to others and that I am not alone—but I also need strength to go beyond me. I need strength to challenge not just how

I was socialized and shaped, but I also need strength to challenge other people and the systems, institutions, and climates that socialize and shape them! I realized that we cannot just cower and take it and brush it off anymore. I need to be brave and strong enough to risk my privileges, and to speak up, engage, resist, and educate. I need that. We need that.

Kalayaan, your name means freedom in Tagalog. You have taught me that we can break free of the ugly legacies of colonialism and modern-day oppression. You have taught me that we can break free of stereotypes and expectations imposed on us by society and even science. From you I realized that we need to free ourselves from the imposed limits of the past and the present. We need to free ourselves from the traumas of the past and their many negative consequences that persist to this day. We need to heal from the unhealthy legacies of colonialism.

And by healing the damages inflicted by oppression on our roots, we end up strengthening our roots. Through this healing, remembering, and empowering, the positives and resiliencies will come to balance, perhaps even outnumber and overwhelm, the negatives. The joys, smiles, laughter, and love will balance out—perhaps even drown out—the desolation, pains, cries, and hate. Through you I realized that we need to be able to imagine a world that is better; conceive a world that goes beyond our conventional ways of doing things—our typical solutions. We need to liberate our minds, hearts, and souls. You have taught me that we can and need to flip the colonized script. I need that. We need that.

Kaluguran, your name means love in our Kapampangan language. You seem to be perpetually smiling, and you seem to have complete trust in people. You still have no suspicions, doubts, fears, or ill will. It looks to me that everything you do is driven by nothing but pure, uncorrupted bliss. And by looking at you I realized that I can use some of that. With as much pain and unfairness our Peoples have been subjected to, it is not only understandable but also natural to hate back, to extract revenge, to be ethnocentric, and to retaliate with violence. For a very long time I was in this ethnocentric—or *Filcentric*—state, and my actions—in those rare times that I was brave and strong enough to do something—were driven by dark, negative, vengeful, even hateful energy.

Don't get me wrong: I want to make sure you understand that it is normal for Peoples who have been maltreated, wronged, marginalized, and oppressed to be in this state. By all means—my children—be angry, be mad, be agitated, be livid! But I sure hope you don't just stay in that state, because this ethnocentric state and the actions that are driven by the hate it creates can be very dangerous, and a tragic example of this is what happened to your twenty-one-year-old cousin and his father—your uncle.

My children, around two years ago in an Athabascan village, two Alaska state troopers showed up at your uncle's house to arrest him. Based on stories and news reports, your uncle has never recognized the authority of the State of Alaska or the United States of America, so he resisted and told the troopers they have no jurisdiction, which is consistent with his long-held belief that the State of Alaska has no rights in Native villages. According to the recorded audio of the tragedy, your uncle said, "I don't believe in this justice system. This is total subjugation. You people came into this country, and we're subjugated." A struggle between your uncle and the two troopers ensued, and your cousin—who was inside the house—took a gun and killed the troopers. Just last month, your cousin was convicted of two counts of first-degree murder and is most likely going to be sentenced for life in jail.

My Filibascan children, your cousin was seemingly raised with consciousness and connectedness. His parents seemed to be aware of the colonialism and oppression the Koyukon Athabascan Peoples have experienced and are still experiencing. It seemed to me like your cousin was raised connected to the culture—fishing, hunting, trapping. Such consciousness and connectedness is what I want for you too—Malakas, Kalayaan, and Kaluguran—but you need to have more than that. You see, in your cousin's and uncle's case, the consciousness and connectedness seems to have sparked only a sense of loss, trauma, pride, vengefulness, and violence, but apparently nothing more. Such dark elements sparked strength and resistance, and obviously a strong desire for freedom. But the actions of resistance and desire for change were not driven by love. Instead, they were driven by anger and hate.

Indeed, according to the news reports, your uncle was a "radical" and your cousin was "taught to hate law enforcement by his father, who is a member of an antigovernment organization named Athabascan Nation." News reports state that your cousin was "saturated in vitriol and hate by his father," who raised your cousin to "despise and fear law enforcement." If Isla Vista is an example of how damaging it is to internalize the oppression we experience, then your cousin's story is an example of when our consciousness of our oppression results only in anger, hate, and resentment. It is an example of when we are not able to move beyond such dark elements, and when such elements are the ones that fuel our found strength and the ones that drive our desire for freedom. You see, the danger in becoming aware of generations of systemic oppression and unfairness is that it can lead to violence toward the oppressors or people who represent the oppressive systems. So although consciousness, connectedness, strength, and freedom are important, they are not enough! They can lead to dark elements and the actions that result from these dark elements are not only ineffective, they can also be very harmful to ourselves, to our communities, and to others. So we need more.

And love is another one more.

Your pure trust in the world, Kaluguran, has thought me to remember love. Now that I see the need to help facilitate collective consciousness and connectedness with other Peoples who share similar struggles, now that I see the need to go beyond just freeing myself but to also extend that freedom to others, I also see the need for my efforts to be driven by love. The actions that are sparked by consciousness and connectedness, and facilitated by strength and the desire for freedom, cannot be effective if they are not driven by love. We cannot effectively help to facilitate systemic, institutional, and cultural changes if our efforts are driven by anger, bitterness, and hate. I cannot be as transformative as I want to be—as I need to be, *as we all need to be*—if I am driven by hostility, resentment, and animosity. Instead, I need to be driven by love.

As Martin Luther King Jr. said, "Returning violence for violence multiplies violence, adding deeper darkness to a night already devoid of stars. Darkness cannot drive out darkness: only light can do that. Hate cannot drive out hate: only love can do that." Even James Baldwin said, "The really terrible thing . . . is that you must accept them . . . You must accept them and accept them with love. For these innocent people have no other hope. They are, in effect, still trapped in a history which they do not understand; and until they understand it, they cannot be released from it." Yes, my Filibascan children, we need to give them love even when all we've received is hate. It seems wrong. It seems contradictory. It seems unfair. But I trust that I need it. I trust that we need it. I need to trust.

I don't want you all to think, however, that all we need is love—like that one song says. I wish it were true, I wish it were that simple and easy, but unfortunately it is not so for Peoples of Color like us. Yes, we need to be driven by love as we try to survive, heal, and make this world better. But my children, we cannot simply have blind, naive, uncritical love. We cannot be blind to the injustices and disparities that our Peoples have faced because of the color of our skin, our worldviews, our languages, our cultures, and our ways of doing things. We cannot be blind to how deep and widespread oppression's damages have been. We cannot be blind to the wounds and the infections. We cannot be blind to how oppression has destroyed, damaged, and weakened us. We cannot be blind to the chains. We need to be conscious and aware of our historical truths and contemporary realities. We need to see our connectedness to other Peoples, especially communities who share similar struggles as us. We need to continue to be strong and to break free from the harmful legacies of oppression. Yes, we need love, but it is not all we need. We also need consciousness, connectedness, strength, and freedom; we need all of them. We need all of us.

Malakas, Kalayaan, Kaluguran—perhaps what you have is what I was searching for, or at least parts of what I was searching for, I don't really know. But what I do know is that these new elements have provided me with something beyond consciousness and connectedness, and have brought me some clarity, peace, and hope—at least for now.

I am sure this world will destroy me again. Oppression is redundant, remember? So I will be depressed again. I will feel terrified, angry, hopeless, and resentful again. This world will make me feel like I need to resort to violence again. But when those moments come, I will have more tools. In addition to consciousness and connectedness, I now also have strength, freedom, and love.

Will these be enough? Probably not. But it's more than what I previously had.

Will I always remember these in perpetuity? Probably not. But now you are here to remind me.

✦ ✦ ✦

My family—our roots are our protection, our shield. And we need to know, understand, and connect with our roots. We need to have consciousness and connectedness. We need to have a shield.

But we need a strong shield. Although our shield is rusted, weakened, and damaged by centuries and generations of oppression, we can work toward repairing our shield's imperfections. Let's balance out—even outnumber and overwhelm—the inflicted flaws and blemishes with the positives and resiliencies of our Peoples and our roots. In fact, let's work toward ridding our shield of its imperfections and rusts—its weaknesses, damages, and vulnerabilities. Let's fix them, heal them, and be liberated or freed from them. Let's develop a shield that is as "perfect" and "flawless" as possible, while simultaneously making sure we are aware of and understand the battles that the shield has been through. So that we know the factors that the shield is up against. So that we know of the factors that have been trying to destroy the shield, factors that have been trying to destroy us. So that we know what the shield has been protecting us from. So that we know that the shield can withstand a lot. So that we know how strong it is. So that we will appreciate its value, its resilience, its magic.

And because *we* are privileged enough to not only still have a shield but to also have developed a relatively strong, solid shield, let's share this shield with others who may not be as privileged as we are. Let's share our developed consciousness, discovered connectedness, remembered strengths, and liberated souls with others. Let's use this to not just benefit and transform ourselves, but to also help transform oppressive systems, institutions, and communities. But in our efforts to do this, we cannot be driven by anger, resentment, or hate. Don't get me wrong, it's ok, understandable, logical, and even therapeutic to feel such things. But we need to be able to get past them if we want to extend healing transformation beyond ourselves. Our efforts need to be driven by love.

And, you see, something magical may even happen once our shield becomes infused with love and when our efforts to share our shield becomes driven with love. Our shield—our roots—may transform into something beyond a protective factor. Our shield may transform into something beyond a defensive tool. Our shield can become an instrument to create instead of just to cover. It can become a mechanism to spread love instead of just something to keep out hate. In fact, it can become a foundation on which we can build a much more just society. If strengthened, healed, and driven by love, our roots can become our salvation.

My family, our roots were damaged. Our ancestors were traumatized. They are not without faults. They are not perfect. Our ancestors had to do what they had to do to survive—and survive they did! And because they figured out a way to survive, we are here today! Continued survival despite generations of attempted extermination is already a commendable rebellion against oppression. But to go beyond mere survival to also become conscious of the truth and become connected to others who share similar struggles provide the rebellion with even more power. To have the strength to resist the continued oppression of our roots today and to break free from the ugly legacies of historical traumas make the rebellion simultaneously adaptable, relevant, and deeply entrenched. And now, to have our fight be driven by love makes the rebellion even more formidable.

We don't have a lot, my loves, but we do have a few things right here among us. I am sure there are many other elements that need to be present for continued healing and social change, but among us we have consciousness, we have connectedness, we have strength, we have freedom, and we have love. And we can make the best of these elements and use them to hold up our roots, the roots that in turn will protect us and hold us up. We have the elements to help us remain steadfast in our personal and collective efforts to heal from the injuries of historical and contemporary oppression. We have the elements to share, leverage, and risk our privileges. We have the elements to help us in our struggle to make this world a better place.

I hope, and I trust, that these elements will help heal us and our damaged roots. In the very least, I hope—and I trust—that these elements will carry us through our time in this world and better position the next generation toward healing.

Our Yup'ik elder, Grandma Rita Blumenstein, has taught us that we are our ancestors. So when we heal ourselves, we also heal our ancestors and their wounds that have yet to heal. Therefore, when we heal ourselves, we also heal the future generations.

You see, as Peoples of Color, we're just connected that way.

We are connected to our ancestors and our relatives—past and present and future—in a very deep, real way. This is not a metaphorical, mystical connection. It's tangible. It's visible. You can feel it; all of it!

You can feel the pains, but you can also feel the joys.

POSTSCRIPT

People get used to anything. The less you think about your oppression, the more your tolerance for it grows. After a while, people just think oppression is the normal state of things. But to become free, you have to be acutely aware of being a slave.

—Assata Shakur,
Assata: An Autobiography
(2001)

Kalayaan's drawing of the family on March 2017.

February 9, 2017

This day last year was Pum's last day alive.

My Filibascan family, so much has happened since.

His family, his community, his friends were all forced to say good-bye to him. We honored him. We buried him. I helped carry his casket and lower his body into the ground. I helped throw dirt onto his grave.

Since then, we've all been trying to deal with Pum's death in our own ways. Some of us have come to be at peace with it. Many of us, including me, are still bothered by it. I will most likely continue to be affected, angered, and devastated by it. Forever. This is how it should be—I think. I don't ever want to be at peace with something so violent. I don't ever want to be fine with something so wrong.

I guess we all just dealt with the tragedy differently. Some of us turned to God, some turned to family, some turned to forgiveness. Some of us turned to other things that are not as healthy. Some are still searching for something to turn to.

Me, I turned to the world. This is because I know that Pum's case is not unique. I know that there are many other tragic examples around us—heartbreaking experiences that happened or are still happening to other families, other communities, other Peoples—that are largely driven by unacknowledged prejudices and violence in the individual, institutional, and internalized levels. Sure, not all forms and

instances of oppression always lead to immediate death—
although way too many do—but oppression always leads
to pain and suffering and, eventually, death. Remember,
oppression is not dead; oppression is deadly.

So I turned to the world. And as I expected, the world
showed me oppression. It showed me pain and suffering. It
showed me death. And in a twisted way, I found solace in
being reminded that I am not alone in this oppression. As
what's been happening for years, it was consciousness and
connectedness—kamalayan and kapwa—operating once
again to give me comfort.

After Pum's death, I saw the battle at Standing Rock
begin to intensify. My Filibascan family, the broken trea-
ties, the land grabbing, the disrespect of tribal sovereignty,
the destruction of indigenous lands, and the extraction of
resources from Native Peoples make this a clear example
of colonization. This is colonialism happening today.

The shooting at a nightclub in Orlando also happened,
when forty-nine people were killed and fifty-three others
were wounded. Given that the vast majority of victims
were gay and Latino, this looks like an example of racism,
xenophobia, anti-LGBTQ attitudes, and toxic masculinity
at the interpersonal, institutional, and internalized levels.
These are all happening today.

And, my loves, more has happened since.

I saw the United States presidential campaigns heat
up. The Republican nominee proposed to "suspend immigration from areas of the world where there is a proven
history of terrorism against the United States, Europe, or
our allies"—essentially a campaign promise that is rooted

in Islamophobia and xenophobia. Even if we use the most stringent definition for what is meant by "areas of the world" to mean just those considered by the U.S. State Department as "Terrorist Safe Havens" or "State Sponsors of Terror," the list of countries to be banned still numbers fifteen: Somalia, Mali, Syria, Libya, Egypt, Iraq, Sudan, Lebanon, Iran, Indonesia, Malaysia, Afghanistan, Pakistan, Yemen, and the Philippines. And as an immigrant from the Philippines, I got very concerned, because approximately 36 percent—one out of three—of the 546,000 nonimmigrant visas, and 43 percent—nearly one out of two—of the 85,000 immigrant visas, that are issued to these fifteen countries every year are to Filipinos.

You see, my Ate and my two nieces were three of the thousands of Filipinos who were issued nonimmigrant visas back in 2007 so they could attend my wedding. My mom was one of the thousands of Filipinos who were issued immigrant visas back in 2006, so we can finally be together after being apart from each other for twelve years. My brother and I—as children—were two of the thousands of Filipinos who were given immigrant visas back in 1994, so we could finally be reunited with our father after being apart for our entire lives. My father was one of the thousands of Filipinos who were given immigrant visas back in 1982, so that he could find better opportunities for his family. And my uncles, aunts, and grandfather were some of the thousands of Filipinos who were issued visas in the 1960s and 1970s.

So, my Filibascan family, the Republican presidential candidate's campaign promise to ban people "from any nation that has been compromised by terrorism" worried me because I saw it as potentially affecting millions of people—Filipinos and our non-Filipino kapwa. I was worried that families would be separated, that their reunification would be delayed if not halted altogether. I was worried that those seeking better chances and breaks in the United States so they can help their families will be denied their shot. I was worried that families like ours will be valued less, treated differently, and denied opportunities simply because of stereotypes and prejudices about their religion and national origin.

And, my loves, much more has happened since.

The Republican nominee for president also bragged about assaulting women and being entitled to do so. I heard the audio recording, and I saw the video. I saw rape culture being propagated by a person who is one election away from becoming the leader of our country. I saw blatant sexism and misogyny happen.

I saw the presidential election happen.

I remember that night, and the morning after. I couldn't sleep and ended up staying awake all night. But as disappointed, tired, and terrified as I was due to the election results, I tried to remain calm and to go through our normal morning routine. As is our daily route, Kalayaan was the first to be dropped off. When we got to her school, I helped put her backpack on, and we did our usual good-byes.

High five. Pound. Foot pound. Hug.

After hugging, I looked her in the eyes and felt the need to say, "Hey, you are capable and you are free to be whatever you want. No one can force you to do anything you don't approve of."

Kalayaan, you said, "Yup, I know, Daddy. Just like you always tell me to remember five things: work hard, practice, never give up, keep trying, and have fun!" I nodded, smiled at you—proud that you remember our mantra well—and watched as you walked into your school grounds.

As I made it back into the car and thought about what just happened, a strong shadow of sadness came over me and I broke down crying. I felt like such a liar. I just lied to you, my daughter—to your face—and it dawned on me that I had been lying to you for years.

You see, our good-byes that morning reminded me of my previous battles with inauthenticity when, as a newly arrived immigrant, I tried to shed myself of my Filipino-ness and pretended to be someone I'm not, just so I could be accepted in this country. Similar to my naive belief when I was younger that all I had to do to become successful was transform myself into someone that this society deems acceptable, I was telling you that it's all within your control and that you are the only one responsible for your success or failure. I was telling you that you just need to learn as much as you can, work as hard as you can, and you will get what you deserve and that you will be treated with equal respect. I was telling you that you are free.

Kalayaan, I have been telling you that this is a just world. And I have been lying to you, my daughter, on behalf of this oppressive world because the reality is that this world's standards of acceptability, respectability, and desirability are constantly moving targets for marginalized people—especially for women of color like you.

My love, I was terrified for our daughter that morning, because the truth is that our daughter still cannot become anything she wants—even if she believes that for herself and even if she's the most qualified and capable.

The truth is that it's not all within her control—not even what happens to her own body.

The truth is that she's still not completely free to become what she wants and doesn't want.

The truth is that equality is still just an illusion.

So that morning, while directly looking into our daughter's eyes, I propagated a cruel myth. And I realized that over the years, despite my consciousness and efforts to resist internalizing the oppression around me, I have nevertheless been reduced to being a vessel of oppression—passing on this illusion of justice, freedom, and fairness to our daughter.

I am sorry, my love, that even though it is already 2017, this is still the kind of world that our daughter must navigate. I am so sorry, Kalayaan.

And, my Filibascan family, so much more has happened since that morning.

I saw that many people were shocked and surprised by the election results. I wasn't. Yes, I was devastated, but not surprised. For those who were stunned, I think their shock is rooted in their belief that oppression is now gone—or at least no longer as prevalent. Many were asking: How can someone so bigoted be elected as president? How can millions of Americans still vote for such an openly and blatantly bigoted person? The answer is easy: It's oppression. It's racism. It's sexism. It's ableism. It's heterosexism. It's Islamophobia. It's misogyny. Things that have been around forever; things that have been redundant. Things that have been deeply rooted and widespread.

Nothing new.

But many people still resisted the explanation that it was oppression that is to blame. Many people resisted the notion that the reason America elected a blatantly racist, sexist, ableist, misogynist, xenophobic, and Islamophobic person for president is because America is still all of these things. Many people instead say that it's the economy, and that the White working-class was the difference in the elections—that the White working-class is just tired of being poor. Many people say that if we fix the economy then the White working-class will feel better and care once again about our "identity issues." This kind of reasoning tells marginalized peoples like us that our basic humanity is not on the same level of importance as theirs. It tells us that our basic right to live and survive is not as important as their desire to prosper and thrive. It tells us that our basic human right to exist is not as important as their perceived right—or destiny, or entitlement—to be above us. And people fail to see that this is exactly what oppression is.

Nothing new.

My Filibascan family, people seem to not realize that this is not just "identity issues" or mere "identity politics." For us, this is an issue of our humanity, our core. So essentially, the White working-class has determined that our humanity is an issue that is not as important as the economy; that our basic humanity is not as important as their economic stability. This line of thinking tells us that White people still tie our humanity to economic issues, essentially saying that they will tolerate us, accept us, or care about us as long as they are economically comfortable, as long as our presence here contributes to their wealth. It tells us that our humanity is still tied to how prosperous they are. A monetary value has been attached to our humanity. My Filibascan family, this has been the history of oppression, playing itself out again. Today.

Nothing new. Even though so much has already happened.

The fact that Peoples of Color, immigrants, women, LGBTQ people, non-Christians—especially Muslims—and other marginalized groups are still not regarded as equal or as human as those who are White, native born, male, heterosexual, or Christian is clearly seen in the aftermath of the election. After 60 million people gave bigotry and hate a pass—after 60 million people loudly proclaimed that social group oppression is tolerable, acceptable, or not as important as the economy or whatever else they claim as their reason for voting the way they did—there was a sharp increase in the country in hate crimes, harassment, and intimidation based on social group membership! Over 1,000 incidents in a month, my loves, and those are just the ones that are reported.

My Filibascan family, plenty of things have happened over the past few months that seem to have given people permission to oppress. Many folks seem to have become highly emboldened to express their prejudices, like they were finally given permission to openly mobilize and act on their long-suppressed, hidden, and simmering hate. Because of this, it has definitely become even easier to be aware of the oppression happening around us.

And I felt connected to the people being subjected to them; I felt a connection to our kapwa. Sure, for a moment,

I felt a sense of desolation, similar to how I felt after Pamiuq died; I felt defeated, depressed, and hopeless again. I felt fear and terror. I felt anger and outrage. I felt ashamed too. Malakas, Kalayaan, Kaluguran—I am appalled that your generation and those who come after you will look at this time in history and ask how we—the adults of today—allowed this to happen. It was embarrassing. What happened over the past few months is shameful.

But I've also learned some things to be proud of over the past few months; the three of you, my Filibascan children, reminded me of the need to go beyond myself and to act. The three of you have taught me the need for strength, freedom, and love. And so as devastating as this period was, it also became an opportunity for intergenerational healing. I also wanted the three of you to look back at it and see that your parents didn't give up. I wanted the three of you to look back to this time in history and see that your parents—your ancestors—did something.

So your mom and I went to Standing Rock three months ago. There are several reasons why we went there. For sure, the movement in Standing Rock is about clean water, clean energy, and the environment. But we should never forget that fighting 500-plus years of colonialism, genocide, and racism are huge parts of the movement too. And so your mom and I went there to resist oppression. We went to Standing Rock so it's clear to you that your ancestors fought. So that you see that your ancestors are strong, and that they struggled for freedom while being driven by love.

As a Filipino immigrant—a settler—in these lands, I went there also because the same idea of manifest destiny that was used to steal lands away from our Native American brothers and sisters is the same manifest destiny that was used to justify the colonization of my Peoples. I went there because the same notion of benevolent assimilation wherein our Native American brothers and sisters were forced to attend boarding schools to erase their culture was the same benevolent assimilation that was used to miseducate Filipinos and inculcate Filipino minds with notions of American superiority.

I went there because, as an immigrant—as a settler—on these lands, I acknowledge that I am not indigenous here. In fact, many of my 3.5 million Peoples are recent immigrants to these stolen lands. So it is important that I pay respect to the indigenous Peoples of these lands, empathize with them, and stand with them as they continue to resist the colonization of their lands and the oppression of their culture. This is why—as an immigrant and as much as I advocate for immigrant rights—I can never say things like "We are all immigrants" or "This is a nation of immigrants." Not only are these statements inaccurate—the three of you, your mom, your ancestors are not immigrants to these lands at all—I also don't think we should advocate for immigrant rights at the expense of further erasing the First Peoples of these lands. And as a Filibascan family, we must know this and we must act according to this.

So Malakas, Kalayaan, Kaluguran—I went there because my Peoples share a similar struggle with our Native brothers and sisters today in terms of fighting against continued colonialism, cultural genocide, and racism. I went there because I now see the truth that my struggle for equality as an immigrant person of color is tied to—perhaps even dependent on—my Native brothers' and sisters' quest for respect, remembrance, and equality in their own ancestral lands. This is because as an immigrant to these lands, how can I expect to be treated with respect and dignity if those who are truly indigenous to these lands are not? As a colonized man, I went there because I wanted to help my ancestors and continue their fight—to help them heal. And as a parent of Filibascan children, I went there because I wanted to set a good example for you—to help you heal. Remember, as Peoples of Color, we're just connected to our ancestors and future generations that way—a very deep, tangible way.

And, my loves, even so much more has happened since.

For instance, two months ago in Virginia, a Filipina restaurant employee who served a group of White teenagers received this message as her "tip": "Build that wall, Trump Daddy!" Their hate blinded them so much that they failed to recognize that she's Filipina and that Filipinos do not cross a wall to get here; we cross the Pacific Ocean. More egregiously, just last month in Las Vegas, a woman was recorded on video spewing hateful words toward her Filipino neighbor. "Go back to where you came from! We don't want you here!," she yelled. The woman told the Filipino man that he is from "some piece of shit Manila-ass, fucking ghetto, living-under-a-tarp piece of shit land." She further called Filipinos "stupid, orange savages" who are "just one fucking generation out of the jungle, like fucking loincloth wearers!" She went on to shout that Filipina women are nothing but sex workers, that Filipinos do nothing but populate the world with "trashy people" who suck resources out of America, and that Filipinos should be thankful to America for colonizing, civilizing, and protecting the Philippines.

Nothing new.

Just a few days ago, the promised travel ban happened, at least for seven of the fifteen countries considered "Terrorist Safe Havens" or "State Sponsors of Terror." The Philippines was spared from the ban, for now. But given that the White House chief strategist and the United States attorney general both have long histories of racist, Islamophobic, and anti-immigrant behavior, it wouldn't be surprising if more oppressive policies are introduced in the coming days. This is nothing new, my Filibascan family. American history is full of discrimination, injustice, and unwelcoming treatment of immigrants. Remember the Nationality Acts of 1790 and 1870 that limited the right to naturalization only to "free Whites." Remember the Chinese Exclusion Act of 1882—the first law to prevent a specific ethnic group from immigrating to the United States. Remember the Mexican Repatriation during 1929 to 1939 that forcefully deported approximately 1 million people of Mexican descent—most of whom were United States citizens. Remember the Tydings-McDuffie Act and the Filipino Repatriation Act in the 1930s that shipped Filipinos in the United States to the Philippines and prevented Filipinos—even those who were American born—from entering the United States. Remember the unjust incarceration of Japanese Americans during the early 1940s. Remember the National Security Entry-Exit

Registration System that was in effect until December 2016 that required males who are over sixteen years old from twenty-five predominantly Muslim countries in Asia and Africa to register with the Department of Homeland Security. My loves, it is clear from these examples that American xenophobia—this unfounded fear of foreigners, immigrants, or people from other countries—has existed for centuries! American xenophobia is an American tradition.

Nothing new.

So yeah, a lot has happened over the past year. This world continues to show us oppression. It continues to show us pain and suffering. It continues to show us death. Like I said, oppression is redundant. It's nothing new. So expect it. Be ready. But please, don't get used to it. Don't habituate to it. Don't put up with it. Don't accept it.

Be fed up with oppression, my loves. Be sick and tired of it! Be angry. Be outraged! Be devastated by it—it's natural to be distressed by something so violent and wrong. I have been devastated by it—many times. In fact, I am even permanently damaged by it. Yes, my loves, I know that we are resilient. I understand that. I believe that. Our Peoples have proven our resilience over and over again, throughout history! The issue is not our resilience; the issue is oppression! Why do we have to keep proving that we can survive and succeed despite significant adversities? Why do we have to keep proving how resilient we are? Why can't the world just get rid of the adversities? Why can't the world just stop oppressing us? Our resiliency should never be in doubt, my loves. Our resiliency is a fact. But remember that our resiliency is not permission for others to keep oppressing us.

So my Filibascan family, be fed up with oppression. Stand up. Speak up. Do something.

And over the past year, it seems to me that a lot of people are fed up. My loves, there seem to be a lot more people now who are driven to speak up, act, organize, mobilize, and look for solutions.

I don't have any solutions; I don't know enough to come up with any. But I do have one suggestion: Whatever solution it is that we pursue, I hope it's not framed or packaged as an "economic" issue. As I've alluded to before, we cannot—we must not—equate our humanity to money. This is what those in power want to do, and we cannot succumb to it.

Framing our struggles simply as an economic issue tells oppressed peoples that we're tolerable as long as those who are in power are comfortable and wealthy. It tells us that we are nothing but economic assets in this country, instead of human beings who should be regarded as core parts of the American family. It tells us that our worth is conditional, that it is based on the extent to which we fulfill the purpose imposed on us by society—which is to contribute, to work, to serve.

But once things get difficult, marginalized peoples are scapegoated, forgotten, thrown under the bus. We are reminded that we are secondary—perhaps even tertiary—to our oppressor's prosperity.

This is the danger of "packaging" the fight for marginalized peoples' rights in terms of how much money or "economic value" we contribute to this country. Because people start seeing marginalized peoples' value and purpose as only that—to contribute to the economic wealth of the country. And so once the economy starts to suffer, especially for White folks, then marginalized peoples—especially peoples of color and immigrants—become dispensable.

If we start courting and compromising with our oppressors, trying to get their support by emphasizing the economy instead of our core humanity and dignity—our identity—then we are just selling out. As marginalized peoples, we are selling ourselves short—very short. Our worth as human beings is way more than how much we contribute to the wealth of this country. Our worth as humans is worth way more than how much we pay in taxes. Our worth as humans is way more than our "spending power." Our worth and basic dignity as humans is way more important than the economy. Our worth as humans is worth just as much as theirs.

The core of our societal problems is the oppression of our core. It just makes sense, therefore, that whatever solution it is we try to pursue should have the valuation and strengthening of our core as its core. Our core humanity should be the core of the solutions. This should be the frame, this should be the package. Nothing less.

Otherwise, oppression will just keep on happening. Plenty of things will happen, but things will still remain the same for marginalized peoples. Oppression will evolve, it will be dressed up, and it will be called other names, but it will still be oppression.

Some people will say that we just need to take little steps toward addressing that core. That "economic" packaging is just a step, a means to an end. People say it's strategic, because it will hit people "where it hurts the most"—and to people in power it's their pockets or bank accounts where they don't want to hurt. My loves,

I understand this approach, and have seen this approach implemented over the years. But I am not sure we can do this anymore, or at least we cannot do just this anymore, because such compromises become precedents that are used to justify the continued disregard of the core—our core. Such "small steps" or strategic efforts are used as evidence to support the notion that addressing the core is not that important—or not as important as addressing other issues that our core has been "packaged" with. Such "small steps" or strategic efforts continue to relegate our core to the periphery—as supplemental issues—instead of being the fundamental issue, instead of being the core. Such "small steps" or means to an end become the layers under which oppression is able to continue hiding, evolving, surviving, inflicting pain, and killing.

So no more "packaging" our humanity along with the economic advantages and value that we bring along. The package should be us—our core humanity—and that should be enough. It shouldn't have to be packaged with anything else that is of value. Our humanity alone should be valuable enough. It should be important enough. This is what we need people to realize. This is what we need people in power to see. They don't see this because they don't see their own core, their own humanity. They've lost it. And so they can no longer be hurt through it. They've come to value their pockets and bank accounts the most, and have become most protective of their wealth, because they've come to see their value as humans—and their superiority over others—as depending on such wealth. So it has become the case that their wealth is where they are hurt the most. But my loves, what should hurt the most shouldn't be their pockets or their bank accounts. What should hurt the most should be their hearts, their humanity, their core that they've lost and the core that they've denied us.

And, my loves, this need to recover their humanity—their core—is key for America, specifically for White America. Remember when I told you that America is not perfect, that you are not perfect? That's not me being mean; that's just the truth. And there should really be nothing threatening about that statement. It's only threatening if you think you are perfect—which is a delusion. So it's only threatening if you are delusional. And my loves, White America has been delusional for generations.

White America is now realizing that they are not special, that they are not above others. They are finally waking up from their generations-long delusion that it is their destiny or noble duty to teach, civilize, and enlighten the world. White America is finally seeing the reality that they are not exceptional, that they are not superior, that they are the same as everyone else. And White America is scared. White America is anxious. White America is threatened. They have never lived on equal footing with others. They've never seen themselves as equal to others. In contrast, we as Peoples of Color are used to this connectedness and interdependence. In fact, it's our worldview; it's kapwa. For White America though, equality is completely against their worldviews of independence, of competition, of manifest destiny, of benevolent assimilation, of White man's burden. So White people are scared, my Filibascan family, and they are lashing out. For generations now, they've bought into their individualism, their perceived exceptionalism, their supposed superiority. They've been without kapwa for a very long time. And it is their duty now to find it, to strengthen it, to see the world through it, and to live according to it. That's their job. Finding their kapwa is the White people's burden.

Until White people get their kapwa back, then I am afraid oppression will continue. It will still be redundant. It's going to keep inflicting pain and damage on us. It will continue to cause pain and suffering. It will continue to bring destruction and death.

And oppression will continue to negatively affect us, our family, our Peoples. However, isn't this a normal reaction to something so violent and wrong? Isn't it normal to be bothered and distressed by generations of destruction? I don't ever want to not be affected by this oppressive world. I don't ever want to tolerate oppression, to habituate to it, to become desensitized to it. I don't ever want oppression to be normal. My loves, we cannot succumb to it and adapt to it. We cannot grow to no longer care. So yes, I am affected by it—I should be. As damaging as it may be for me, for us, I am glad I am bothered by oppression.

I don't ever want to be at peace with something so violent. I don't ever want to accept something that is so unwelcoming. I don't ever want to be fine with something so wrong. I don't ever want to become accustomed to something so oppressive. My loves, we need to be affected, to be bothered, to care, to want better. For our ancestors. For our children. For us.

BIBLIOGRAPHY

Alaska Department of Corrections, "2015 Offender Profile." Juneau, AK: Author (2016). Accessed July 18, 2016. http://www. correct.state.ak.us/admin/docs/2015profile.pdf.

Alexander, Michelle, *The New Jim Crow: Mass Incarceration in the Age of Colorblindness*. New York: The New Press, 2012.

Baker, Bryan, and Nancy Rytina, "Estimates of the Unauthorized Immigrant Population Residing in the United States: January 2012." United States Department of Homeland Security Office of Immigration Statistics (2012). Accessed March 15, 2017. https://www.dhs.gov/sites/default/files/publications/ Unauthorized%20Immigrant%20Population%20Estimates%20 in%20the%20US%20January%202012_0.pdf.

Baldoz, Rick, *The Third Asiatic Invasion: Migration and Empire in Filipino America, 1898-1946*. New York: New York University Press, 2011.

Baldwin, James, *The Fire Next Time*. New York: Vintage, 1993.

Bulosan, Carlos, *America Is in the Heart*. Seattle, WA: University of Washington, 1973.

Bureau of Justice Statistics, "American Indians and Crime: A BJS Statistical Profile, 1999-2002." Washington, DC: United States Department of Justice (2004). Accessed July 18, 2016. http://www.bjs.gov/content/pub/pdf/aic02.pdf.

Chae, David H., Amani M. Nuru-Jeter, Nancy E. Adler, Gene H. Brody, Jue Lin, Elizabeth H. Blackburn, and Elissa Epel, "Discrimination, Racial Bias, and Telomere Length in African-American Men." *American Journal of Preventive Medicine* 46 (2014): 103-11.

Choy, Catherine Ceniza, *Empire of Care: Nursing and Migration in Filipino American History*. Durham, NC: Duke University, 2003.

Coates, Ta-Nehisi, *Between the World and Me*. New York: Spiegel and Grau, 2015.

Cordova, Fred, *Filipinos: Forgotten Asian Americans*. Dubuque, Iowa: Kendall/Hunt, 1983.

David, E. J. R., ed., *Internalized Oppression: The Psychology of Marginalized Groups*. New York: Springer, 2014.

——, *Brown Skin, White Minds: Filipino/American Postcolonial Psychology (with Commentaries)*. Charlotte, NC: Information Age Publishing, 2013.

Deloria, Vine, *We Talk, You Listen*. New York: MacMillan, 1970.

DuBois, W. E. B., *The Souls of Black Folk*. New York: Dover, 1994.

Dunbar-Ortiz, Roxanne, *An Indigenous Peoples' History of the United States*. Boston, MA: Beacon Press. 2014.

Duran, Eduardo, *Healing the Soul Wound: Counseling with American Indians and Other Native Peoples*. New York: Teachers College Press, 2006.

Duran, Eduardo, and Bonnie Duran, *Native American Postcolonial Psychology*. Albany, NY: State University of New York, 1995.

Enriquez, Virgilio G., *From Colonial to Liberation Psychology: The Philippine Experience*. Manila, Philippines: De La Salle University Press, 1994.

Espiritu, Yen Le, *Home Bound: Filipino American Lives across Cultures, Communities, and Countries*. Los Angeles, CA: University of California Press, 2003.

Evans-Campbell, Tessa. "Historical Trauma in American Indian/Native Alaska Communities: A Multilevel Framework for

Exploring Impacts on Individuals, Families, and Communities." *Journal of Interpersonal Violence* 23 (2008): 316–38.

Fanon, Frantz, *The Wretched of the Earth*. New York: Grove, 1965.

Freire, Paolo, *The Pedagogy of the Oppressed*. New York: Continuum, 1970.

Ignacio, Abe, Enrique de la Cruz, Jorge Emmanuel, and Helen Toribio, *The Forbidden Book: The Philippine-American War in Political Cartoons*. San Francisco, CA: T'boli Publishing, 2004.

Indian Health Service, "Fact Sheet: Disparities, 2016." Accessed July 18, 2016. http://www.ihs.gov/newsroom/factsheets/disparities/.

——, "Fact Sheet: Behavioral Health, 2015." Accessed July 18, 2016. https://www.ihs.gov/newsroom/includes/themes/newihstheme/display_objects/documents/factsheets/BehavioralHealth.pdf.

LaFromboise, Teresa, Hardin L. Coleman, and Jennifer Gerton, "Psychological Impact of Biculturalism: Evidence and Theory." *Psychological Bulletin* 114 (1993): 395-412.

Lakota Peoples Law Project, "Native Lives Matter." Santa Cruz, CA: Author (2015). Accessed July 18, 2016. http://www.docs.lakotalaw.org/reports/Native%20Lives%20Matter%20PDF.pdf.

Meaney, Michael J., and Moshe Szyf, "Environmental Programming of Stress Responses through DNA Methylation: Life at the Interface between a Dynamic Environment and a Fixed Genome." *Dialogues in Clinical Neuroscience* 7 (2005): 103-23.

Memmi, Albert, *The Colonizer and the Colonized*. Boston, MA: Beacon, 1965.

Nadal, Kevin L., *Filipino American Psychology: A Handbook of Theory, Research, and Clinical Practice*. New York: Wiley, 2011.

Napoleon, Harold, *Yuuyaraq: The Way of the Human Being.* Fairbanks, AK: University of Alaska, 1996.

National Partnership for Women and Families, "Alaska Women and the Wage Gap." Washington, DC: Author (2016). Accessed July 18, 2016. http://www.nationalpartnership.org/research-library/workplace-fairness/fair-pay/4-2016-ak-wage-gap.pdf.

Neblett Jr., Enrique W., Deborah Rivas-Drake, and Adriana J. Umana-Taylor, "The Promise of Racial and Ethnic Protective Factors in Promoting Ethnic Minority Youth Development." *Child Development Perspectives* 6 (2012): 295-303.

Ocampo, Anthony Christian, *The Latinos of Asia: How Filipino Americans Break the Rules of Race.* Stanford, CA: Stanford University Press, 2016.

Reyes, Barbara Jane, "Women of Color and Body Politics." *Harriet: A Poetry Blog* (2011). Accessed July 18, 2016. http://www.poetryfoundation.org/harriet/2011/04/women-of-color-and-body-politics/.

Royal Canadian Mountain Police, "Missing and Murdered Aboriginal Women: A National Operational Overview." Author (2014). Accessed July 18, 2016. http://www.rcmp-grc.gc.ca/pubs/mmaw-faapd-eng.pdf.

Ryan, William, *Blaming the Victim.* New York: Vintage, 1971.

San Juan Jr., E. "We Charge Genocide: A Brief History of US in the Philippines." *Political Affairs* (2005). Accessed July 18, 2016. http://www.politicalaffairs.net/we-charge-genocide-a-brief-history-of-us-in-the-philippines/.

Sciutto, Jim, Tal Yellin, and Ryan Browne, "The Massive Implications of Trump's Muslim Travel Ban in 5 Maps." *CNN Politics* (2016). Accessed February 9, 2017. http://www.cnn.com/2016/06/15/politics/muslim-ban-maps-donald-trump/.

Shakur, Assata, *Assata: An Autobiography*. Chicago, IL: Lawrence Hill Books, 2001.

Southern Poverty Law Center Hatewatch, "Update: 1,094 Bias-Related Incidents in the Month Following the Election." Author (2016). Accessed February 9, 2017. https://www.splcenter.org/hatewatch/2016/12/16/update-1094-bias-related-incidents-month-following-election.

Strobel, Leny Mendoza, *Coming Full Circle: The Process of Decolonization among Post-1965 Filipino Americans*. Quezon City, Philippines: Giraffe Books, 2001.

Sue, Derald Wing, *Microaggressions in Everyday Life: Race, Gender, and Sexual Orientation*. Hoboken, NJ: Wiley and Sons, 2010.

University of Alaska Anchorage Justice Center, *"Intimate Partner Violence and Sexual Violence in the State of Alaska: Key Results from the 2015 Alaska Victimization Survey."* Accessed July 18, 2016. http://justice.uaa.alaska.edu/research/2010/1103.05.avs_fy15/1103.051a.statewide_summary.pdf.

Walters, Karina L., Selina A. Mohammed, Tessa Evans-Campbell, Ramona E. Beltran, David H. Chae, and Bonnie Duran, "Bodies Don't Just Tell Stories, They Tell Histories: Embodiment of Historical Trauma among American Indians and Alaska Natives." *Du Bois Review* 8 (2011): 179-89.

Wolf, Leon, *Little Brown Brother: How the United States Purchased and Pacified the Philippines*. New York: Oxford University Press, 1992.

ABOUT THE AUTHOR

E. J. R. DAVID, Ph.D., is of Tagalog and Kapampangan heritage, and was born in the Philippines. He grew up in Pasay, Las Pinas, and Utkiagvik, Alaska. He obtained his bachelor's degree in Psychology from the University of Alaska Anchorage (2002), and his master of arts (2004) and doctoral (2007) degrees in clinical-community psychology from the University of Illinois at Urbana-Champaign. He is an associate professor of psychology at the University of Alaska Anchorage, where he also directs the Alaska Native Community Advancement in Psychology Program. Dr. David has produced three books, *Brown Skin, White Minds: Filipino/American Postcolonial Psychology, Internalized Oppression: The Psychology of Marginalized Groups,* and *The Psychology of Oppression.* He was the recipient of the 2012 American Psychological Association Minority Fellowship Program Early Career Award in Research for Distinguished Contributions to the Field of Racial and Ethnic Minority Psychology, the 2013 Asian American Psychological Association (AAPA) Early Career Award for Distinguished Contributions to Research, the 2014 Alaska Psychological Association Cultural Humanitarian Award for Exemplary Service and Dedication to Diversity, and the 2015 Fellow Status by the AAPA for "Unusual and Outstanding Contributions to Asian American Psychology." He lives in Anchorage with his wife, children, and countless relatives and friends.

Bartering in Pum's house when E.J. visited Barrow, Alaska in 2012.